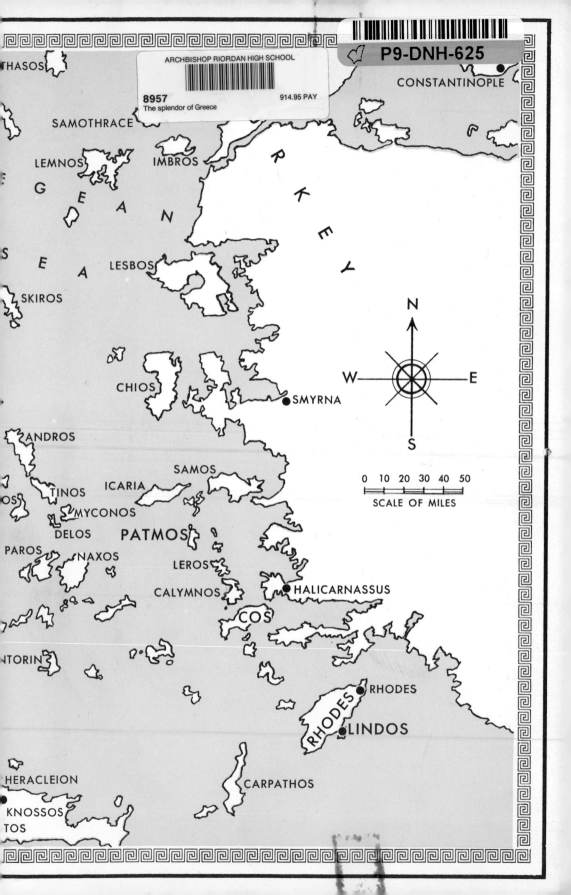

THASOS

SAMOTHRACE

LEMNOS   IMBROS

G
E   A
E   A   N

SEA

LESBOS

SKIROS

CHIOS

SMYRNA

ANDROS

SAMOS

TINOS   ICARIA

MYCONOS

DELOS   PATMOS

PAROS   NAXOS   LEROS

CALYMNOS

COS

HALICARNASSUS

NTORIN

RHODES
RHODES

LINDOS

HERACLEION   CARPATHOS

KNOSSOS
TOS

TURKEY

CONSTANTINOPLE

N
W   E
S

0 10 20 30 40 50
SCALE OF MILES

THE SPLENDOR OF GREECE

THE SPLENDOR

BY ROBERT PAYNE

HARPER & ROW, PUBLISHERS

OF GREECE

NEW YORK, EVANSTON, AND LONDON

FOR
ALIKI AND POL
Χαίρειν

CONTENTS

ILLUSTRATIONS

THE SPLENDOR OF GREECE

I   THE SPLENDOR

The traveler visiting Greece for the first time is shocked by the barrenness of the land. Except for a few weeks in spring there are no exuberant colors, no warm and rolling landscapes such as we find in southern France or northern Italy. Once the mountains were thickly wooded, but now most of them are naked. It is a hard land, where men must live close to the earth, and even today they live very much as they lived in the heroic age. The thin black goats give them milk and cheese and meat; they have wine and olives and fish. They still trap birds in nets, and they still seek for wild honey. There are only a few fertile patches; the deserts of rock are everywhere.

This naked rock is bathed in a naked light—a light unlike any other light on the surface of the earth. It is a light that can be drunk and tasted, full of ripeness; light that filters through flesh and marble; light that is almost palpable. It fumes and glares, and seems to have a life of its own. It is in perpetual movement, flashing off the sea onto the rocks, flashing from one mountain to another and back again, spilling over the valleys. There are only a few places—the plain stretching north of Peking and the foothills of the Elbruz mountains in Persia are others—where light has the quality of being almost sentient, so that one feels its breath on one's face. It crowds the heavens, it shouts, it exults. It is a living thing: so living that the Greeks gave it the physical presence of a god and called it Phoebus Apollo, the god of the divine radiance, and they chose for his birthplace the small bare island of Delos set in the deep purple seas of the Aegean.

The Greeks never tired of describing the appearance of light. They especially liked the glitter of moist things, stones and sand washed by the sea, young bodies emerging from water, fish churning in the nets. They chose for the site of the temple to Apollo at Delphi two beetling rocks called the Phaedriades, the Shining Ones, very crisp and clean, and always moist from the mountain springs. To the modern eye these rocks rise bare and threatening over the valley, but to the Greeks they were comforting. They were containers and givers of light, a suitable habitation for Apollo after his long journey by sea.

The Greeks spoke of "the rosy-fingered dawn," but beyond those fingers were hands, arms, shoulders, a face. The whole body of Apollo poured across the sky, intensely virile, flashing with a million points of light, healing everything it touched, germinating the seeds and defying the powers of darkness. He was not the sun only: he was the moon, the planets, the Milky Way and the faintest stars; he was the sparkle of waves, the gleam in eyes, the glistening of bleached cloth, and the shining of a girl's face. He was the strange glimmer of fields on the darkest nights; and whenever a spring issued from a mountain, he was present at the moment when it emerged into the light.

He was not the most powerful of the gods, but the one who gave the greatest blessings, the most generous and the most far-seeing. From him came order and the definition of things and clear outlines. He was the painter who splashed color on the sky and mysteriously turned the orange rocks to purple in the evening. His constant companion was the dolphin, the sleekest and shiniest of all creatures.

When Homer wanted to describe the goddess Athene, he called her "the bright-eyed one," and when he wanted to depict Helen walking along the ramparts of Troy, he did not describe her face or how she walked; it was enough to say she wore a shining veil. For Homer, as for the Greeks, almost everything that was shining was holy. Light was the sap of life; and if one must die, it is best to die in the sun:

> Make the sky clear, and grant us to see with our eyes.
> In the light be it, though thou slayest me!

So Ajax prays to Zeus in the *Iliad*, a prayer which wells up from the very depths of the Greek consciousness. The same prayer, stated in the briefest possible way, became the cry of the Greek soldier in battle: *"Aëra!"* which means air, wind, sky and all the spaces above the luminous earth.

There are places in Greece which seem to have been made of crystallized light, of light so intense and pure that it seems more real than the objects it embraces, as though light itself had form and shape and substance. There is a moment at dusk when everything becomes bathed in a pale transparent light, in a pure limpid glow, which is so theatrical that you feel you could leap into the sky and go swimming there, and this is especially true of the cities near the sea and the islands of the Aegean, which seem to be no more than jumping-off places into the habitable sky.

But it is at dawn that you see light in its most tangible form. It leaps from the sun and crashes against everything it touches. It puts on its most ceremonial garments, shouts deliriously, quivers, dances, parades itself in magnificence and stamps across the surface of the earth with an almost human grandeur: Apollo visiting the holy shrines every day of the holy year, robed in the colors of the dawn.

Apollo remains; and it is unlikely that he will ever completely disappear, for he is the most prevalent of the gods. Zeus hides in Olympus, Athene has her special shrine in the Parthenon in Athens, Dionysus comes only at the time of vintage, but Apollo is present wherever there is light. At night he vanishes, and then the Greeks are miserable. No other people keep so many lights burning at night, and even during the brightest days they like to have the electric light turned on. Light is their solace against the evil dark.

The Babylonian and Assyrian gods were heavy and earthbound, larger than life but still belonging to the world of nightmares. The animal-like features of the Egyptian gods speak of grotesque encounters with the powers of darkness. The Greeks were the first to give their gods the colors of sunlit flesh, and it pleased them to place the gods in the upper air, or on the high mountains, or arising from the shining sea spray. For them the goddess of love was not a many-breasted matron, but a young virgin arising out of the waves. There is a sense in which they invented virginity: fresh and clean and full of promise like the coming of each day.

Not, of course, that there were no dark gods in Greece. They had their dragons and their serpents, creatures who lived out their ghostly lives in the dark bowels of the earth, relics of an earlier dispensation. The memory of these ancient gods survived, and sometimes it was necessary to placate them. The great ivory and gold statue of Athene on the Parthenon showed the grey-eyed goddess standing guard over Athens, calm and youthful, superbly in command; but a snake twined around her shield and the leering head of the ancient Gorgo hung at her breast, and both of these derived from an age long before Athene came to birth. Hercules killed the Centaurs and buried them deep below the island of Myconos, but they still haunted men's minds. Apollo slew the Pytho, but the priestess who uttered his prophecies and the games held in his honor were all named after the monster.

The ancient Greeks had no illusions about the depths of darkness in the human soul. At night especially the soul was at the mercy of its haggard imaginings; and evil things crept out of their holes. They wove their magic spells, mixed lovers' potions, and existed, as all men have always done, on the edge of superstition. Yet they refused to permit superstition to ride roughshod over them. They were essentially creatures of light, believing that the lucidity of the mind could put an end to the darkness of the soul.

Believing in light, they could not escape the belief that they were sharers and partakers of the divine radiance. When Protagoras wrote that "man is the measure of all things," he did not mean that men were the masters of their fate; he meant that all things were possible to men who believed in the gods, and that men were the gods' regents on earth. In the words which Plato attributes to Protagoras: "Man has a share of the divine attributes, and he was the first of all creatures to know the gods, because he alone possessed kinship with them, and raised altars and made images of them." To the Greeks, Bergson's famous thesis that "the universe is a machine for the making of gods" must have been almost a commonplace.

But all this came about slowly, and we know almost to the exact day when the Greeks, after centuries of fumbling, saw themselves for the first time as creatures shining in a divine light. This event occurred after the battle of Salamis. On that warm summery day, September

23, 480 B.C., the power of Persia on the Greek mainland and in Greek waters was utterly destroyed. Within a year the liberation of Greece was complete.

For fifty years, until the death of Pericles in 429 B.C., the Greeks lived, thought, built temples, sculpted and painted as though they were the natural children of the gods. A prodigious strength moved in them. In the space of two generations, with extraordinary rapidity, they set out to conquer the furthermost regions of the human spirit, and they progressed so far that all the works of art and literature composed since that time are hardly more than footnotes to the vast page they wrote. They set the course of western civilization. In those fifty years, without any apparent sense of strain, like men going about their daily affairs, they established an empire over the mind so enduring that we remain their willing prisoners.

When the great Arab philosopher Ibn Khaldun set out to study the rise and fall of civilizations, he noted that they all rise and fall in the same way, obeying ineluctable laws. He noted that it sometimes happens that a civilization will come into existence as the result of a divine visitation, and it also happens that a civilization about to perish from corruption will be suddenly revitalized by another divine visitation. So Islamic civilization arose from "the divine energy" of the prophet Mohammed, and continued only because at periodic intervals men appeared charged with the same energy. Something very like a divine visitation seems to have occurred in Greece.

Quite suddenly the sky seemed brighter, the earth more beautiful, men's minds moved faster and their eyes saw farther and their supple bodies were equipped with unsuspected powers. The Greeks themselves seem to have been a little surprised by their sudden lucidity. It was as though all the long years of nightmare were over, and at last they stood in the clear light of day. "Where others see but the dawn coming over the hill," says Blake, "I see the sons of God shouting for joy." The Greeks regarded themselves as the sons of God, and the echo of their joyful shouting can be heard down the ages.

Who were they? What kind of men walked through the streets of Athens and Olympia and Delphi? Would we recognize them if we met them in the street? What moved them to create so much, so fast, and so beautifully? What were the whips that drove them on, and what were the reins that held them back? Why did they perish?

We know these men well, for they left abundant records which have survived by a series of happy accidents; and if Caesar or another had not set fire to the library of Alexandria, and the Crusaders had not destroyed the libraries of Constantinople, we would know them even better. The surviving records are not so many as we would like, but more than enough to satisfy our most urgent needs. We have lost nearly all their music and most of the works of their major dramatists and lyric poets; we have none of their mural paintings, and none of the great chryselephantine statues which were the peculiar glory of the age. But we have enough temples, enough statues, enough philosophy and history and poetry to permit us to see them at a close view. If for example the contents of the great library formed by King Eumenes II at Pergamum had survived intact, it is possible that we would stagger under the weight of the vast literature they produced. Time seems to have chosen well; it has left the best.

With the help of marble busts and two thousand pages of Plato and two score pages of Xenophon we can see Socrates plain. There is a very small marble portrait of him in the British Museum which shows him standing in his usual attitude of quiet contemplation, his chest and one arm bare, his robes wrapped loosely and untidily around him; but what is remarkable is that the portrait destroys the image of the snub-nosed, satyr-like demon of comic ugliness we have learned to recognize. The satyr vanishes. Instead, we see a man with a forehead like the prow of a ship and a searching gaze, an upper lip as long and heavy as Shakespeare's, holding himself with a natural elegance. It is a face to ponder on, for he did more to advance the frontiers of knowledge than any man.

Socrates stands at the forefront, but there were others of towering eminence. In that miraculous fifty years a great galaxy of brilliant men walked in the streets of Athens. The architects Ictinus, Callicrates and Mnesicles; the sculptors Phidias, Alcamenes, Cresilas, Polyclitus and Paeonios; the philosophers Democritus, Protagoras and Anaxagoras; the physician Hippocrates; the poets Pindar and Bacchylides; the dramatists Aeschylus, Sophocles and Euripides; the historians Herodotus and Thucydides; the generals Cimon, Themistocles and Pericles. Only a few were native Athenians. Herodotus came from Halicarnassus, and Hippocrates from Cos. Polyclitus came from Argos. Democritus and Protagoras came from Abdera in northern Thrace, a town where the inhabitants inexplicably had a reputation for stupidity. Anaxagoras came from Clazomenae in Asia Minor. Pindar was born in the town of Cynoscephalae or "Dogs' Heads" in Thebes, and Bacchylides on the island of Ceos. Aeschylus came from Eleusis, and Euripides from Salamis, where he was born on the very day of the victory against the Persians.

This splendid muster roll represents the triumph of the Greeks, not of the Athenians only. When Greece was liberated, a wave of excitement ran through all the colonies in Asia Minor and Sicily. They were intoxicated with freedom. They had caught a glimpse of Persian magnificence, and suddenly it seemed to them that the commonest Greek peasant who had taken part in the battles was the equal of the King of Kings.

They had won their most devastating battle at sea, and it is therefore not surprising that when Sophocles celebrated the unique achievements of man, he gave seamen the place of honor:

> *Many marvels there are,*
> *But none so marvelous as Man.*
> *Over the dark sea he rides*
> *In the teeth of the winter storm,*
> *Driving through towering spray.*
> *While the oldest of gods, the Earth,*
> *The hoary, the indomitable one,*
> *He wearieth year by year*
> *With the turning of the plowshare*
> *Drawn by the patient mules*
> *Over the endless furrows.*

Command of the sea gave them a fierce pride of empire and a sense of unity with all the scattered colonies stretching from Asia Minor to Sicily and the coasts of Africa. They were free now to adventure in whatever direction they pleased, and since men possessed a share in the divine attributes, they felt they could climb Olympus and tear down the veils which separated the gods from men. They were in a Promethean mood, and like Prometheus they were to suffer agony.

These agonies however were reserved for a later time. For the moment they were free to celebrate as they had never celebrated before. The first precise statement of their joy in freedom which has survived was made by the unknown Aeginetan master who carved the figure of the crouching soldier in the lion helmet on the pediment to the temple of Aphaia. He is all quivering nerve and muscle, leaning back a little only to be able to shoot his arrows more accurately. The battle of Salamis was largely won by the Aeginetan archers and swordsmen, who butchered the Persians in the narrows. It is possible that this young archer is a portrait of the Aeginetan commander Polycritus, who, when he saw Themistocles coming up after the battle, taunted him with the cry: "Now do you think the people of Aegina are friends of Persia?"

The temple of Aphaia was the only temple known to have been erected specifically in honor of the victory at Salamis, but there is a sense in which all the great temples constructed during the next fifty years were memorials of that victory. In Olympia, at Delphi and on the Acropolis at Athens the captured shields and weapons were displayed. Salamis—the word seems to be of Phoenician origin, from "shalem," meaning peace—brought to the Greeks a peace almost too great to be borne.

We know this period of fifty years as the classical age of Greece, but it was in fact a fiercely romantic time. The Greeks would have been surprised if they had known they would be credited with the virtues of calmness and order and deliberate self-restraint. Calmness there was, but there was always an unresolved excitement close to the surface. We have been misled too often by plaster casts in school and the sterile light in museum galleries: seen in the sunlight those statues quiver with suppressed excitement. Those faces are not impassive, and they are rarely austere. The maidens who take part in the procession of the Panathenaea move with incomparable grace, but they are the faces of ripeness and eagerness; the young horsemen are telling bawdy jokes to one another; there is always awe and sometimes terror in those long processions. Time has smoothed out the features, as it smooths the faces of the dead; and this is all the more reason for studying the sculptures which have been well preserved.

Instead of self-restraint, there was an almost total abandonment to experience. Instead of calm there was seething violence, an explosive need to exert all human power to the uttermost. There was some order, but this was imposed by the gods and by the nature of the city-state. Order was the governor which prevented the spinning wheel from being torn apart by its own momentum. "We impose upon ourselves the restraint of reverence," said the austere Pericles in his Funeral Speech. "We are always obedient to the laws and to those set in authority over us." How the enemies of the Greeks must have laughed!

Plato says the Egyptians looked upon the Greeks as children, too young and innocent to be the creators of great things. The Greeks had no pyramids, no kings as splendid as the Pharaohs, no luxuriant Nile to bring fertility to their fields. They had only their hard land and their native intelligence and the quickening light.

The Greeks shaped the new gods in their own image. Hoary old Poseidon, his blue hair streaming on the waves, gave place to Athene, the virgin, who smiled at her friends and threatened ruthless war against her enemies. Apollo, her brother, climbed into the ascendancy and became the rival of Zeus. During the miraculous fifty years when Athens was the center of civilization, Athene and Apollo became the guardians of Greece.

They were the youngest and sweetest gods who ever ruled, lovers of life and of the mind's free soaring flight. They were the harbingers of human freedom against the weight of oppressive tradition. They were the new buds bursting forth in a world rotting with corruption.

In a very short time the great age was over. Perhaps it could hardly be otherwise, for such displays of violent intellectual and artistic energy must have exhausted the Greeks early. Pride sapped at their strength, and the disastrous expedition to Sicily destroyed their faith in themselves until once again, with the coming of Alexander, another "divine visitation" charged them with the energy which led to the conquest of the East, until this conquest in turn lost its original impetus. Yet Alexander's desire to build a world empire in which all men would be citizens derives from Socrates, who claimed to be only a citizen of Athens.

The splendor of Greece still lights our skies, reaching over America and Asia and lands which the Greeks never dreamed existed. There would be no Christianity as we know it without the fertilizing influence of the Greek Fathers of the Church, who owed their training to Greek philosophy. By a strange accident all the images of Buddha in the Far East can be traced to portraits of Alexander, who seemed to the Greeks to be Apollo incarnate. We owe to the Greeks the beginning of science and the beginning of thought. They built the loveliest temples ever made, carved marble with delicacy and strength, and set in motion the questing mind which refuses to believe there are any bounds to reason.

That is why we journey to Greece like pilgrims to a feast.

II MYCENAE

Among the grey ribbed mountains of the Argolid the mind plays strange tricks at times. Seen through the mist and rains the peaks assume the shape of helmeted warriors, charioteers, armies on the march. Gaunt warriors writhe in combat, and dragons creep along the floors of the valleys. Here and there the mountains are slashed with red, like fresh blood. Those mountains, which rise abruptly and meaninglessly, have the appearance of fatality. No wonder the ancient Greeks believed that Hercules performed so many of his labors there.

These are mountains of a heroic temper, with sudden flaring precipices, with no gentleness in them, no softly curving slopes. They have the rawness of power. These jagged ascents were made for heroes. There are almost no farmsteads: only the shaggy goats foraging among stones, and the peasant boys amusing themselves through the long watch by playing on their pipes.

The shapes of mountains tell us much. I remember in the valley of Yenan in northern China mountains shaped like golden tents which resembled the tents employed by Chinese emperors, a form which is imitated in the great palaces in Peking. There are tawny lion-headed mountains overlooking Persepolis whose shapes are reproduced in the writhing lions carved on the portals and stairways. Overlooking Isfahan there is a mountain shaped like a sleeping girl, and for five hundred years the Persian artists have reproduced her graceful contours even when they were painting a vase. I suspect that the shapes of mountains are burned into the minds of the people who live under them, who have fought over them. Sometimes the shapes of mountains can define a whole art.

These mountains guard the northern approaches to the Peloponnese and explain why so many of the battles fought between the Athenians and the Spartans took place at sea. No one in his senses could hope to take them by storm. An army descending the rocky defiles can be ambushed at leisure, and many armies have perished in them, including the army sent by the Turks to quell the Greek rebels under Kolokotronis in 1822. Beyond the mountains lies the plain of Argos once ruled by Agamemnon, "lord of the many islands and all of Argos." One does not have to look far to see why the lord of the plain could control so much of the Peloponnese.

Fuere fortes ante Agamemnona: there were strong men before Agamemnon. But Agamemnon remains the first of the Greeks to stand out in the full light of history. That at least was the opinion of Thucydides, who began his history of the Peloponnesian War with a critical survey of the war against Troy. He was not one of those who are inclined to dismiss Homer lightly. He believed the war took place, and Agamemnon led it, welding his forces together more by the fear he inspired than by the love they had for him. He does not think too highly of Agamemnon's leadership, for the war, he says, lasted for ten years because Agamemnon permitted his forces to disperse and take part in piracy. There were people who doubted whether such a huge expedition could have been organized by a pirate chief living in the small and obscure town of Mycenae. "Then think of Sparta laid desolate," Thucydides replied, "with only the temples and the foundations of the public buildings above ground, then surely as time went on people would refuse to believe she had been powerful and famous."

For Thucydides, Agamemnon was a historical figure, not so large and imposing as Homer and the tragic dramatists made him, but larger than most men. We know him well: arrogant and imperious, a strange stern man of commanding aspect, who believed in dreams and auguries, as most people did in his time, and he suffered from inexplicable rages, quarreling violently with his closest friends. He had the gift of remoteness, and was absent for long periods from the battle. He was not overly brave, and though he led the largest fleet of his time safely into Trojan waters, he seems to have been a careless sailor and lost most of his ships during the return voyage. He was in fact the kind of pirate chieftain who was doomed to be murdered in some backstairs quarrel.

He was not however an ordinary pirate: no cutthroat Morgan whose fleet never amounted to more than a few ships of the line. In his calm way Thucydides points out that Agamemnon must have represented a continental power to have been the master of so many islands. He must have commanded a large fleet. He must have possessed a quite extraordinary ascendancy over his men. He established a naval camp on the shore facing the citadel of Troy, and this in itself, Thucydides thinks, was an achievement of no mean order. Thucydides is curiously silent about the fate reserved for Agamemnon when he returned to Mycenae. The watchtowers are lit. The purple carpet is laid out. The chariot drives across the plain, and Agamemnon falls into the welcoming arms of his wife Clytemnestra only to be stabbed to death a little later. It would be good to know what Thucydides thought about that murder and all the other murders that resulted from it. In his calm authoritative way he would have cut through the legends to give us the living man beneath. It is possible that Agamemnon was murdered, as other pirates have been murdered, for all the gold he carried in his purse.

We came across the shadowed plain of Argos in the driving rain, but the clouds cleared a little and the dappled earth was green again. It was warm and humid: the only humid day I ever knew in Greece. There was no sense of palpable menace, only the sense that there was something strangely familiar about this land, the long low plain, the sharp mountains, the emptiness of the place.

Nearly everyone who comes to Mycenae is struck by a sense of strangeness. It is perhaps a trick of the mind, the knowledge of the curse laid on the family of Agamemnon, but I suspect that it is something more. The earth is a deep rich red, corn and barley are growing on the edge of the village, there are avenues of eucalyptus trees, and everywhere people are going about their ordinary affairs. Goats and sheep are grazing in the stubble. It could be any village in Greece except for the sense that we have reached a frontier, one of those ghostly places where an invisible line is scratched on the earth, and beyond this line all customs and traditions change. We come to the end of a journey.

As the road climbs from the village toward a deep fold in the mountains, there is at first no sign of the great citadel which once dominated the nine-mile plain. The citadel wears her protective coloring well.

Suddenly there is a turn in the road, and there in front of you are perhaps forty feet of cyclopean walls and the Gate of the Lionesses, and the shape of that dark stone across the lintel curiously echoes the shape of the mountains which soar behind the citadel. The faces of the lionesses have vanished, blotted out at some remote time in the past, but there is an an imperial strength in their heavy limbs. Between the lionesses there stands a single column, which perhaps represents the king's golden scepter.

Those vast cyclopean walls have a menace of their own. There are rough-hewn stones like petrified sponges which weigh two tons. There is a strange bleakness and heaviness and forbiddingness. It is a place which says: "I am strong. I will smash anything that crosses my path."

Beyond the Gate of the Lionesses, only a few yards away to the right, are the shaft graves excavated by Schliemann. They are like open graves now, sulphur color, honey color, with black pools in them. They are perhaps ten feet deep, which is deep enough for a prince. Weeds grow in them and round them, and when the autumn rains come the weeds grow knee-high. The graves seem to be waiting for the dead.

Beyond the graves, up the stone stairways, lie the palaces. The rooms are not very large. They give the impression of being scattered haphazardly up and down the ridge of the mountain. The wooden pillars and the roofs have vanished, but the stairways are intact, and what is surprising is that they are rough-carved, not at all like the stairways one imagines in palaces. I suspect that Mycenae was a fortress only, and somewhere out on the plain there were summer palaces to be occupied in times of peace.

Mycenae crouches on the rock. It is still waiting for the enemy.

At some period in a very remote past murders were committed here. In one of those roofless rooms, which are no more than square sheets of rock with hollows for the long-vanished doorposts, Cassandra screamed in terror, having seen the children slaughtered in her dreams, and not far away is the chamber where Clytemnestra and Aegisthus celebrated their guilty loves, and the bath where Agamemnon was murdered, and the place where Orestes was first aware of the flutter of the leathery wings of the Furies. A blood-red sea of evil dashed against these rocks, until every cranny smelled of death. "Death and desolation," says the tutor in Sophocles' *Electra*, "shall visit this house." They did, but what is curious is that the visitation seems to have happened quite recently, within the memory of men still living.

There is no escaping from the spell: the odor of corruption in the air. Except for the monolithic stones and the Gate of the Lionesses there is nothing remarkable here, no splendid courts, no spacious stairways, no great carvings of tribute-bearers in endless procession such as we find at Persepolis. There is only rubble, and here and there the traces of the Dorian burning, and the open graves. And somehow it is very right. The menace is all the greater because it is never completely expressed. We are haunted by a presence which never reveals itself.

Mycenae has changed very little since the day when Heinrich Schliemann drove across the plain with his young and beautiful Greek wife. He was a strange wild-eyed man, haunted by gold, and the way he went about excavating Mycenae has made two generations of modern scientific archaeologists weep with vexation. He tore down walls, dug trenches wherever it pleased him, and rarely took notes. He had read in Pausanias that the graves of Agamemnon and his companions were "within the gates," while those of Clytemnestra and Aegisthus were outside. His mind, moving mechanically and logically—with the terrible logic of the half-insane—fastened on the words of Pausanias, and refused to let them go. He was perfectly prepared to dig up the entire space "within the gates," with or without the permission of the Greek government. Nothing daunted him. For day after day nothing emerged except hundreds of clay cows. He insisted that the clay cows were tremendously important, for clearly they represented "cow-eyed" Athene. He found some fat clay goddesses, and said they were images of Hera, the wife of Zeus, for no reason that anyone has been able to determine.

Day after day under the scorching sun he stormed, raged, cursed and continued digging, keeping at bay the watchdogs assigned to him by the Greek government. He was in no mood to be crossed. Had he not discovered in Troy the diadem of Helen? He had scattered the treasures of Troy in hiding places all over Greece, and it amused him to taunt the Turkish government, which had let the treasure slip through their fingers. Now he was taunting the Greek government, telling them over and over again in letters intended to reduce them to paroxysms of despair that nothing in the world could stop him at his god-given task of bringing into the clear light of day the evidence of Greek greatness. He would show them Agamemnon plain. He would uncover from the earth more treasures than he found in Troy.

When the first strip of ancient gold was uncovered by his spade, he very nearly died of excitement. Because he dared not touch the gold with his own hands, and was afraid that in his nervousness he would somehow destroy it, he sent Madame Schliemann down into the grave pit. For twenty-five days she crouched in the grave, delicately scraping the earth from the gold-encrusted bodies of the heroes with a penknife. She never complained. She, too, was a master of intrigue, and, being hopelessly in love with her husband, she fought the watchdogs with weapons he would never have dared to employ. When at last the graves gave up their dead, armored in gold, crowned with gold, with gold goblets beside them, Schliemann could scarcely contain himself. He sent off telegrams to all the world announcing that the Trojan heroes had returned again at the touch of his magic wand.

After Mycenae he made no more conquests. Like a ghost he

wandered across the world in search of more buried treasure, but the earth, which had given him so much, was already weary of him.

THE FACE OF AGAMEMNON

Today the gold mask which Schliemann discovered in Grave V at Mycenae holds pride of place in the National Museum at Athens. It stands before all the great bronzes which have been found in the sea, and all the massive stone sculptures. In a glass case, set against black velvet, it is the first thing you see when you enter and the last when you leave.

Schliemann would have approved. He would have said he deserved the honor. He would have prowled round the gallery, rubbing his hands at the sight of so many objects he had taken from the earth. There are so many of them that almost it is his gallery.

He found many masks at Mycenae, but none so beautiful as this. He did not think it was the mask of Agamemnon; he found what he thought to be the body of Agamemnon, and the mask over it was a ruined ribbon of gold, quite expressionless. "These masks," he wrote, "are likenesses of the deceased. Had it not been so, all the masks would have been representations of the same ideal type." Of only one thing was he certain: these masks had once belonged to heroes who took part in the Trojan War.

We know now that the masks together with everything else in the graves antedate the Trojan War by six centuries, and we are not so sure that they are "likenesses." Most of the masks discovered in the royal tombs lack recognizable character; they seem to have been fashioned hurriedly, with no desire on the part of the artist to depict the features of the dead chieftain with any accuracy. Only "the beautiful mask" succeeds brilliantly in suggesting the terror and the poignancy of death.

This mask possesses power and authority, and a terrible beauty.

Death is marked on it, but there is no hint of repose. It seems to have been made many days after death, when the flesh has thinned and the skin is drawn taut and corruption is setting in. It is not so much a portrait of the dead man as a portrait of death, sculpted and molded by an artist who has transferred to a thin sheet of gold his own terror before the sight of a decaying corpse. Yet there is more than terror. There is a sense of nobility, of the chieftain's fierce pride continuing into the afterlife. An unearthly beauty shines from him. He wears already, in these last moments of physical existence, a more than human aspect. It is perhaps the portrait of a great warrior at the moment of dissolution when he becomes a god.

It is all done with astonishing simplicity. The eyebrows are etched in with sharp incisive scorings; there is no attempt to depict more than the outlines of the upward-curving mustache. He wears a small goatee, a few hairs below the lips. The wide ruff, which now gives the appearance of a full beard, was tucked under the jawbones and chin. Small holes below the ears show how the mask was attached to the face by a thread passed round the back of the head. The ears are almost abstractions: the same pattern has been found on pottery. Taken one by one the details are unimpressive, yet the whole has a spine-chilling majesty.

When Schliemann found the mask, it was painfully bruised and twisted, and it was not the bright yellow gold that it is now. It had a reddish color, very warm. Cleaned, smoothed out, it has acquired since 1872 almost the brilliance of copper. It is a pity. One would like to have seen it when it shone with a reddish fire.

The mask is a mystery, a pure gift of the earth. Modern archaeologists are inclined to believe that it dates from 1700 B.C., many centuries before the Trojan War, and they are certain that it cannot be earlier than 1400 B.C., because two fragments of Egyptian porcelain bearing the cartouches of Amenophis III, who reigned from 1440 to 1400 B.C., were conveniently left in the grave circle.

Yet it is just possible that they are wrong. It is possible, after all, that this is the face of Agamemnon.

THE TREASURY OF ATREUS

When Schliemann was very old and in search of conquests, his mind
turned toward Crete. For some reason he believed that his excavations
in Crete would crown all his achievements. He was sure there was
buried treasure beneath an olive grove in the hills overlooking Heracleion, and he bargained with the Turkish proprietor of the land.

Schliemann had made four huge fortunes before he set out to uncover the heroes of the Trojan War. He had long experience in
bargaining. He could speak Turkish—he had learned the language
in six weeks—and he thought he knew exactly how to deal with
Turks. He offered to pay 50,000 francs for the land and the olive
trees, and the documents were drawn up. Schliemann asked how many
olive trees there were, and was told there were 2,500. He went out
to count them, found there were only 888, returned in a rage, tore
up the contract and took the next ship for Athens. The glory of
being the first to uncover a Minoan palace fell, not to Schliemann,
but to Sir Arthur Evans.

It was typical of Schliemann in his last years that he should quarrel
over olive trees. He quarreled with nearly everyone, and most of all
he quarreled with himself. He quarreled with merchants, with officials,
with scholars, and with kings. He even quarreled with the Emperor
of Brazil, Dom Pedro II, an amateur archaeologist who made a special
journey from Corinth to Mycenae to view the progress of the excavations.

The Emperor was a young man of impeccable manners and con-
siderable charm. He arrived with a retinue and exclaimed over the
beauty of the objects Schliemann had found—he had not yet found
the gold masks, and in fact he had only some grave steles, fat clay
goddesses, clay cows and innumerable fragments of pottery to show
for his excavations. To honor the Emperor, Schliemann invited him to
dine in the Treasury of Atreus, which lies only a little way from the
Gate of the Lionesses.

The Treasury of Atreus is a beehive tomb, fifty feet high, lined with dark and gleaming stones, some of them as large as the parapet stones of Mycenae. It lies under a low hill, and the colossal doorway was once flanked by two slender pilasters which now stand in the British Museum, for Lord Elgin stole them, as he stole so many other things. They are the color of old ivory, very delicate, and they still bear traces of gold foil. One might imagine these exquisite columns decorating the palace of an oriental princess.

Into this vast, dark and beautifully curved tomb Schliemann brought a table, silverware, horsehair sofas and hanging lamps. He spread carpets on the floor, filled the flower vases with all the flowers his servants could find, gave detailed orders for the preparation of the roast lamb and sweetmeats, and then waited. The Emperor arrived on horseback.

Schliemann was in his element. He sat at the head of the table with the Emperor beside him. His white shirt front gleamed. He discussed learnedly the long history of the excavations at Mycenae, and commented on the fact that only once before had an Emperor entered this tomb, but that was three thousand years ago. No doubt this ancient Emperor was carried in state, a gold mask on his face, his wives lamenting him. No doubt, too, musicians played, and poems were recited. After coffee and liqueurs Schliemann offered his cigar case to the Emperor. They smoked contentedly.

One does not often invite Emperors to dinner. One does not often spread out a feast in an ancient tomb. Schliemann was understandably charmed by his own regal composure as he welcomed the Emperor, who towered over him and who sometimes demonstrated an appalling ignorance of the nature of these excavations. There were protestations of friendship, and Schliemann promised to dedicate his next book to him.

The next day the Emperor set out for a prolonged tour of the Near East.

Schliemann was still very pleased with himself, savoring the memory of the dinner in the tomb, when he learned there was trouble among the Greek police. Police captain Leonardos claimed he had been given a forty-franc tip by the Emperor. The policemen under him claimed he had received a thousand francs, to be shared equally by all the police. Soon they were at each other's throats. Leonardos was so put out that he resigned. When Schliemann heard of the matter he sent off a telegram to Cairo asking Dom Pedro point blank how much he had given to the police. "I beg Your Majesty in the name of the sacred truth and humanity," he wrote, "to tell me the exact amount you gave the police captain." The Emperor seems to have been charmed by the incident. He said he had indeed given only forty francs. Thereafter Schliemann would sometimes be heard muttering about the ingratitude of kings.

Schliemann had excelled himself in the tomb. That vast and curving tomb with its high doorway can still suggest the splendor of a vanished age. There are other beehive tombs nearby, but none so perfectly preserved. These age-blackened walls were once adorned with massive gold rosettes, but now they are naked; and the tomb of the king has gone; and there is only rubble in the small antechamber which once perhaps contained his treasure chests. But there is no other building in Greece which has such perfect symmetry. There is no dread in this place: only the enclosing dark.

One thinks of the tombs of kings all over the world: all shapeless and tunneled, cut into rock faces, attended by heraldic lions. One thinks of the grave pits in Sumeria with the strangled servants and the butchered horses lying around the catafalque of the king. All in their various ways show that they were mortally afraid. Here in the curiously misnamed Treasury of Atreus, who was the father of Agamemnon, there is no fear. Whatever king designed this soaring tomb was conscious of his own splendor and the splendor of his own death.

When we came out of the tomb four yellow butterflies darted down the long lane carved in the hillside. They seemed to spring out of nowhere. They danced wickedly down the lane, and then they floated gaily over the gently sloping hills.

III   PHAESTOS

When Arthur Evans bought the hill at Knossos with the 888 olive trees and established himself as the excavator of the imperial Minoan capital, it was his custom to ride out every morning from his comfortable quarters in Heracleion, and he would start digging soon after sunrise. It was remembered that he whipped the mule very hard, and usually did the journey in half an hour. He looked a little like Schliemann. He was a short, grave, close-fisted man with an aquiline nose and a bad temper. He was rich, ferociously industrious, and he liked to give grandiloquent names to things. He uncovered Knossos, and then did his best to destroy it.

Today you can make the journey from Heracleion to Knossos in a few minutes by bus. It is a pleasant journey along a curving road, with evergreens and red-roofed houses hidden in the smoke of summer. The farm boys are red-faced, and they look healthier and sturdier than the farm boys in Greece. The goats look fatter, and better-kept. After the other Greek islands Crete wears an air of luxuriance.

Knossos appears at a bend in the road, and the first glance at that formidable palaeolithic wall gives promise of excitement. We have read the schoolbooks. We know a little about the legendary sea-king who ruled by the sign of the double ax and watched the youths of his court tumbling over the horns of wild bulls. We have heard of Theseus and how when he returned to Athens from Crete after killing the Minotaur he forgot to reef the black sails of his ship, and his father, thinking he was dead, threw himself from the Acropolis in grief. We tell ourselves that it will be more exciting than Mycenae. There will be delicate pavilions covered with frescoes. There will be a vast stairway leading to the Hall of the Double Axes. We shall be permitted to sit on the throne of Minos and dance on the ancient dancing floor. Knossos, we tell ourselves, will be more evocative than Mycenae. In the delights of Knossos we shall forget the Treasury of Atreus and the Gate of the Lionesses. We shall bathe in the springs of Western civilization.

Unfortunately nothing of the kind happens. There is a palace, but it is a very small one. There are frescoes, but they have all been recently painted. There are beautiful blood-red pillars, but on closer examination they prove to be of reinforced concrete. There are stairways, but I have seen better stairways in poverty-stricken villages in Spain. The site is unprepossessing, though the Cephalonian fir trees are magnificent. The dancing floor consists of a few cobblestones. Something has gone wrong.

A great number of things have gone wrong, for though there is no doubt that Knossos was the palace of Minos, we shall never know what the palace looked like. Evans shored up the ruins, furnished them, decorated them, gave them impossible names and stamped them with his own excessively Victorian imagination. The throne room has no throne; it has a small curiously curved chair which may have been used by a head butler. Behind the chair is a fresco showing some very supercilious seals in a flower garden. At any moment Alice will come running in and asking for the Mad Hatter. Whatever faith one had in Evans' efforts to restore the palace which crumbled at every touch of his spade is destroyed by that Victorian fresco.

Mercifully I had brought *Zorba the Greek* with me. I had half finished the book. I was in Crete, and it was about a Cretan. Alexis Zorba with his fiery eyes and hollow cheeks and his ferocious thirst for experience was a good antidote to the twittering of the guides. I found a patch of shade under a newly painted fresco and devoured the book while the bees hummed and the fir trees sighed in the summer wind.

I do not know what Zorba would have said if he had come to Knossos. No doubt he would have spat and uttered some choice expletives. He was one of those men "who crack life's shell and go straight to the very substance." He would have approved of tumbling over bulls, and he would have cast a sly glance at the maidens who wandered into the bull ring with such an air of presumptuous innocence. He would have said that double axes are admirable weapons for frightening reluctant widows. Zorba had a fine taste in women, though he accused them of stealing the apples from the garden of Eden and stuffing them down their bodices. Far from being descended from Adam's rib, women, he thought, stemmed in direct line from the horns of the Devil.

I read for a while, and then went off to find the grave of Zorba's creator, Nikos Kazantzakis, who is buried near the wall of Heracleion. He was a small man with thick bushy eyebrows and piercing eyes, who somehow combined a gift for living abundantly with the gift of storytelling. He read Nietzsche, and it blew the top of his head off. He studied under Bergson at the Sorbonne, and learned to think calmly. He was nearly always poor, and slept through many winter nights in Paris in a coffin in a museum. He wrote fifty books, and none of them made any money, but he was perfectly content with his life. He roared with laughter, and wept unashamedly. He was already dying of leukemia when he went to China. In Canton, shortly before flying over the North Pole to Germany, he was given an injection by a Chinese doctor. Inflammation set in, and he died a few weeks later in Freiburg. He was the best of the Greeks, and it was good to wander in his happy shade.

THE PAINTED SARCOPHAGUS

Knossos is the ruin of a ruin, and there is very little to be said in favor of Evans as the restorer of an ancient palace. For more than thirty years he dug around the hill, so much in love with the place that he fashioned it after his own dream of what a Minoan palace should look like. The treasures he discovered are now in the new, gleaming museum at Heracleion, together with the other treasures found by Greeks, Englishmen, Frenchmen and Italians.

There are exquisite treasures. Crystal goblets, gold cups, diadems, signet rings, necklaces, earrings, great geometric vases, thimbles, helmets, daggers. In nearly every corner there are double axes, symbols of Minoan power. Unfortunately the black blades have a curious resemblance to tar paper.

Upstairs are the frescoes. They are very odd. Frescoes ten feet high have been imagined out of a few square inches of paint. The Cupbearer, the most graceful of attendants at a royal feast, stretches to the skylights, but of authentic Minoan paint there is barely enough to cover a penny postcard. The Prince of the Lilies is a feathered helmet, a few scattered pieces of chest, and one leg: the rest has been imagined. La Parisienne remains entire, but she is rapidly fading into a murky blue-grey. The Bull-ring fresco has bits of the bull and most of the girl leaping on its back, but the attendant who catches her is only a waist and part of a leg.

One wanders among these frescoes with a sense of bewilderment and loss. Those paintings, so often and so uncritically admired, disintegrate before the eyes. Sir Arthur Evans was clearly faced with a conundrum. There were splashes of paint on the walls, and he was determined, like someone working on a jigsaw puzzle to fit them together. There was a recognizable Minoan style, and so he fitted them together on the basis of a style which had grown familiar to him. There is for example the famous fresco known as the Saffron Gatherer depicting a young boy bending over the saffron in a garden, plucking it and placing it in a basket. It is one of the best of the frescoes, and scarcely stretches the credulity. The boy had no head, but that was a small matter. His strangely twisted body was indigo in color, but that could be explained by the fading of the paint over nearly forty centuries. A Greek scholar examined the fresco carefully, and came to the conclusion that it was not a boy gathering saffron, but a cynocephalic monkey gathering flowers from the flowerpots of one of the royal gardens. The boy and the saffron had both vanished. The Greek scholar explained that he came upon the solution to the puzzle by observing that Sir Arthur Evans had made no allowance for the monkey's tail, which was visibly present in the painting. Sir Arthur Evans thought it was a boy; the Greek scholar believes it is a cynocephalic monkey on no evidence except the presence of the tail; my own feeling is that the little bits of paint can be carefully arranged to form a fairly respectable cat.

It is all very odd, and there seems to be no easy explanation for the perpetuation of the fraud. Sir Arthur Evans once explained how these "restorations" were accomplished. Whenever the excavations seemed to be approaching a wall where frescoes might be found, he would station a Swiss artist in his employment nearby; then as the wall came to light and before the paint disintegrated the artist would quickly make a water-color painting of what he had seen. A few flakes of paint would remain, and these were fitted into the general design established by the artist's painting.

No doubt the artist painted what he thought he saw, or what he wanted to see. No photographs of the frescoes as they first came to light were made, and so we shall never know how they appeared in those brief moments before they crumbled in the sunlight. Afterward came the juggling with little fragments of paint. It is a game which is played without rules, effortlessly, and without taking much thought. The game has been played with varying success in all the Greek ruins where remnants of paintings have been found.

But if the frescoes leave a sour taste in the mouth, the beautiful paintings on the stone sarcophagus found at Hagia Triadha leave only sweetness. The paintings are gay and delicate and at the same time very solemn, for they describe the sacrificial ceremonies for the dead prince who once lay in the sarcophagus. Nothing has been lost, and therefore nothing has been restored. The colors have faded a little, but only a little—there are startlingly fresh madders, rose pinks and emeralds. There is a sense of movement and life, even of joy in life. The sarcophagus dates from a period long before the building of the palace of Knossos, and is therefore the oldest European painting to have survived.

What is astonishing is the sense of immediacy established by the unknown artist. We are drawn into the ceremony, which takes place before our eyes.

On one of the long sides of the sarcophagus a bull tied with brilliant scarlet ropes to an altar has just been stabbed. The blood is dropping into a bucket. A priestess blesses the dying bull, and a procession moves toward the altar surmounted by a double ax. That is all, but the brightness of the blood and the slow march to the altar are wonderfully depicted.

The other side of the sarcophagus is even more mysterious. We see the great two-handled urn which will receive the blood of sacrifice offered by a priestess. There follows a woman with a strange bird-shaped crown, who carries two baskets over her shoulders; these baskets contain the thighs of the bull, which will be burned perhaps on the steps of the columns crowned with the double axes. Behind this woman comes another, the most stately of all, who plucks at a seven-stringed lyre with a plectrum. From these women fall rippling banners in the shape of feathers, announcing they are the servants of the goddess represented by the dark bird.

To the right of the lyre player the scene abruptly changes. Three priests wearing sheepskin skirts are bearing offerings to the dead— two brindled calves and a long curved boat. They are set against a darker background, signifying perhaps a journey into the earth, into the darkness which opens out on a sacred grove where another altar stands. In front of this altar, calm, impassive, stands the dead man, wearing a striped shroud. His feet are hidden, so that he gives the impression of slowly emerging from the darkness at the summons of the priests who come with their offerings.

At one end of the perfectly balanced panel we see the blood of sacrifice falling in the sacred urn, at the other end we see the dead man raising in the sacred grove. As the blood is poured, so life flows in the dead. Unmistakably the panel portrays a resurrection, the long-wished-for return of the young prince who died about 2040 B.C.

On these painted panels there is no confusion, no attempt to over-dramatize the figures. The three women and the three men move with an enviable dignity and grace, with a naturalness which betrays the emotion of the artist. There is solemnity, but there is also a quiet joy in the expectation of deliverance from death. There is the faintest suggestion of Egyptian and Assyrian influences in the stern profiles of the priests, in the long eyes, in the sheepskins belted at the waist, but the women are wholly European, robust, high-breasted, swinging their heavy skirts. The sun of Europe shines on the scene, and we are far from the East.

One can spend hours poring over this painting. How uncluttered it is, compared with the great processional frieze on the Parthenon! How simple, and at the same time how mysterious! Who is the dark woman? Her hair is a tangle of rich curls. Is she a Nubian or an Egyptian? The priests have an Egyptian elegance, but there is no elegance in the white-skinned priestess who bends forward as she pours the blood of sacrifice with a purely European awkwardness. Two cultures seem to be represented on the painting. They have not yet fused, and seem to be a little surprised by the confrontation.

So, perhaps, one can go on forever enquiring into the mysteries of this sarcophagus found in a small tomb chamber near Phaestos. Above and below are fields of flowers, and on the uprights are stars and sunwheels painted with the quick curling lines characteristic of Minoan art. We shall not see those tesselated fields of flowers again until we come to the Byzantine mosaics, and those spinning sunwheels do not reappear until the coming of Islam. Strangely, the panels surrounding the painting suggest the ornate Cappella Palatina at Palermo built three thousand years later. Like a jewel the painting is embedded in a setting of incomparable richness.

There is one final mystery. The dead man rising from the earth in the shade of a tree, dark-faced, still wrapped in a shroud, gazing straight in front of him, stands before what seems at first sight to be an altar or a tomb. On closer examination the lower part of the altar is seen to be filled with waving lines suggesting a fountain, the water of life flowing upward and so balancing the blood which pours down on the left side of the panel. Altar, tomb, fountain—perhaps it is all of these. Perhaps, too, the unspoken words are the same as those which are found on the gold tablet of Petelia, now in the British Museum:

Thou shalt find to the left of the House of Hades a Well-spring,
And by the side thereof standing a white cypress.
Do not approach the Well-spring.
Thou shalt find another by the Lake of Memory,
Cold water flowing forth, and there are guardians before it.
Say: 'I am a child of Earth and of Starry Heaven,
But my race is of Heaven alone. This ye know yourselves.
And lo, I am parched with thirst and I perish. Give me quickly
The cold waters flowing forth from the Lake of Memory.'

PHAESTOS

That morning Apollo was raging. The sky was spread out like an immense blue sail flapping in the hot wind, and the dust rose, churning over the fields of brown wheat stubble and the carpets of green grapes left out to dry. The bus roared across the island, choking and groaning, and throwing up plumes of black smoke. "Phaestos!" the driver shouted, and he pointed toward a blue mountain which seemed to be made of ice.

We roared through the small town of Gortys and drowned it in dust. The banana trees were dry and withered, but the olives were mysteriously fresh and green. On the windshield the driver had hung three sacred images to protect him as he skimmed on two wheels round corners—a silk butterfly, a porcelain eye, a gilded cross. Strange medley of images! To the ancient Greeks the butterfly represented the soul, and the eye of heaven came from Egypt, and the cross from Palestine, which is not far away.

The sunlight in Crete is thicker, milkier, even more robust than in Greece. It does not sting, as on the island of Delos. It comes with tremendous force, but gives an impression of slowness, even of heaviness. One waits for it to relent, but it does not relent. Scattered over the fields are shelters of woven reeds, for the patient donkeys and cows.

The blue mountain came closer. A very old mountain, with the ribs showing through, scarred with the white crusts of wounds. There was something gravely majestic about the way the mountain swept upward toward its peaks. "Zeus!" the driver shouted, and then I knew it was Mount Ida, and there, near the summit, like an eye patch, lay the Cave of Zeus.

It is in fact many caves, one cave leading to another, and recently a Greek archaeologist explored it again and found some battered shields and the rusty blades of ancient swords and a handful of gold ornaments. It is not a difficult climb, but I had no intention of going up there in the heat.

Phaestos mercifully has a guest house which permits you to look down on the ruins and over the wonderful plain of Messara without staying for long in the sun. Knossos is something of a fraud, a deceptive and ingenious reconstruction, with fresh paintings on the walls and raw, red pillars made only a few years ago. Phaestos, excavated by the Italians, is authentic to the last stone and the last broken column.

The plain of Messara sweeps majestically to the sea, a breath-taking site for a city. The ruins are bleak and bare, as they should be. There is only stone: stone piled on stone—stairways, theaters, palaces, altars. This city is older than Knossos, and may be the oldest of all European cities. Sir Arthur Evans found a small stairway in Knossos, about five feet wide; he called it the Great Stairway. At Phaestos there is a stairway forty feet wide, and no one has troubled to give it a name.

There is spaciousness here, the sense of abundance. Everything is in the open. There are no underground passages and tortuous labyrinths. The city stands on a rock looking toward the Bay of Messara and the brightly carpeted valley. Knossos suggests a delicate aristocratic country house, the summer villa of one of the minor princes. Phaestos suggests royal power.

There are no histories of Phaestos, no collections of the songs sung by her poets, no written records except the tablets engraved in linear B with their lists of furnishings—laundry lists would be more useful. There is the famous stone disk with delicate stamped ideograms, the earliest example of printing, but no one knows what it says. It is very dark and very small, and stands now in the museum at Heracleion on a little pedestal, and could easily be overlooked. Occasionally among the ruins of Phaestos you come upon the signatures of the builders, stars, moons, planets, set amid curious lettering, but they are indecipherable. There are only a few references to Phaestos in Greek literature. Homer speaks of the ships leaving the harbor— "their blue prows borne to Egypt by the strength of wind and wave." He knew the harbor well—"at the time of the south-westerly gales the great rollers drive towards a headland hard by Phaestos, where only a small reef holds them back." Idomeneus, King of Crete, returned to Phaestos after the Trojan War, but he remains as shadowy as Minos.

This strange city lying beneath the cave where Zeus was born, all ruin and desolation beneath the bare scorching sky, still has power to move us. There is grandeur in its emptiness, the sun flashing silver off the stones. There is none of the low chattering from the past which can be heard in Knossos: the delicate paintings, the fountains splashing in the courts, portraits of beautiful boys. Like Mycenae and Olympia, Phaestos has no need for decoration. The power of the ancient scepter still radiates from the citadel.

IV   O L Y M P I A

One hot summer day about the year A.D. 100 the rhetorician Dio Chrysostom, the friend of the Emperor Trajan, found himself wandering along the banks of the Alpheus. He was alone, and he had lost his way. He wandered through a forest, where there were no pathways, and afterward he came out into a rough plain where there were altogether too many paths—sheep paths, goat paths, paths leading to cattle pens. It was all very confusing. With no one in sight, and the heat growing stronger every minute, he decided to climb a small hill, where there was a clump of oaks, and from there he hoped to find a house where he could rest during the afternoon.

He found no house. Instead he found a heap of ruins, the stones piled carelessly together, the drums of the broken columns scattered among the oaks. The temple, which once crowned the hill, had fallen apart, but the shepherds still worshiped there. He saw the still-fresh skins of the sacrificed animals hanging up, and there were shepherds' crooks and the clubs with which they defended themselves from wild beasts, and these he believed to be their offerings to the gods. He had been there only a little while when he saw an old woman sitting on the ground. When she rose, he saw that she was unusually tall and strong, and very old, with long grey hair. He asked about the animal skins and the clubs, and she answered in a broad Doric accent that the place was sacred to Hercules, and she was the priestess of the ruined temple. She had the gift of second

33

sight, and all the farmers in the neighborhood came to ask her about their crops and cattle. Dio Chrysostom thanked her, and went on to Olympia, where there was another temple which had not yet fallen into ruins.

That obscure temple in the oak grove tells us a good deal about the survival of the ancient cults, and especially about Hercules, whose influence was spread over all this flat northern part of the Peloponnese. The temples fell into ruins, but the gods survived, and the priests and priestesses still attended to their worship even when there were no more statues of the gods. It was enough to hang a shepherd's crook on a tree, and to flay a goat. And if all the stones had crumbled away, the shepherds would still come with their offerings.

The visitor to Olympia today is in the same position as Dio Chrysostom. He sees only a shapeless ruin, stone piled on stone, a litter of crumbling stones in a grove of pine trees, and the light flickering through the pines gives a strange unreality to the scene. No old priestesses sit among the ruins. There is only a terrible barrenness, and the knowledge that the gods have departed.

The great gold and ivory statue of Zeus has gone. The sacred olive tree, called "the olive of the beautiful crown," from which the slender olive boughs were cut with a golden sickle to be twisted into crowns for the athletes, has gone, and no one knows where it stood. The temples have crumbled away, and so have the gymnasium and the hippodrome, and the stadium where the sacred games were held lies under twenty feet of earth.

Once it was the most sacred place on earth. All the great princes of Greece attended the games, and the tyrants of Italy and Sicily came in gilded barges and were rowed on the swift-running Alpheus almost up to the walls of the sacred enclosure. Aeschylus, Sophocles, Euripides and Pindar recited their poems here; Herodotus read his histories aloud; Thucydides wandered through the lanes of marble statues. Here even the gods took part in the games, for the record of victors includes Apollo, who outdistanced Hermes, the messenger of the gods, at running, and outboxed Ares, the god of war.

Every refinement of sculpture and architecture was employed to make Olympia worthy of the gods and of the victors in the races.

Unfortunately there were no marble quarries in the neighborhood, and the temple builders were forced to use a rock consisting of millions of seashells, which they covered with stucco and polished with marble dust. Stucco and marble dust have long since perished. Everywhere you tread there are seashells flaking away.

The shining cliffs at Delphi announce the presence of a god, but the low curving hills around Olympia suggest only a great calm. One would expect to find a temple to a goddess, perhaps to the mother of the gods, for here everything is as resolutely feminine as Delphi is masculine. At some ancient time long before history Olympia was the seat of worship of the moon goddess Hera, and Pausanias remembers a legend which tells how the Olympic games originated in a foot race run by girls for the privilege of becoming her priestess. There were of course many other legends. Pindar says categorically that Hercules was the founder of the games. He measured off the sacred grove in honor of his father Zeus, and ordained that all the plain around should be given over for rest and feasting and games, and gave the name of Kronos to the hill which overlooks the sanctuary in honor of the ancient god who was overthrown by his father.

We shall never know how the games came into being, or why so many gods were crowded into the sanctuary. The two neighboring cities of Elis and Pisa claimed possession of the site and waged war for the right to control the games. It would seem that they agreed for the sake of peace to place all their gods in Olympia, and share them with all of Greece. In 776 B.C. the Olympic peace was established. In the summer of that year the games were officially opened, and for the Greek historians it was the beginning of history. Henceforth all dates were to be marked as so many years after the opening of the games.

Something of quite extraordinary moment had occurred, for the opening of the games for all the Hellenes implied the possibility of peace among all the tribes in Greece. For the first time they envisaged a reign of peace under the auspices of the gods. With peace came order and elegance and pleasant rivalry. For the games men traveled under safe-conduct from the remotest regions, and there arose, as always happens under similar circumstances, a vast traffic in ideas. The games were far more than a substitute for war; they provided the impetus from which Greek civilization came into being.

In the beginning there was only the sacred grove, the race track, the temples to Hera and Zeus and the local gods. The temples were small, made of wood. Gradually, as wealth poured into the treasury of Olympia, the buildings were made larger, and after about 600 B.C. the wooden columns as they rotted away were replaced with stone. Pausanias, who came to Olympia nearly a thousand years after the games were inaugurated, noted that there was no uniformity in the columns. On one temple there would be many different kinds of columns, some of stone, some of wood. Inside the temple of Hera there had been preserved an ancient column, presumably from the first temple erected there.

Every fifth year the sacred heralds set out from Elis and made their way across Greece to proclaim the truce. They were ambassadors from the gods, and therefore treated with the utmost respect. The truce was rarely broken. Once the Spartans broke the truce and made war against Lepreum; they were heavily fined and excommunicated. So sacred was the festival that even when the Persians were launching an attack on Greece, the games continued as usual, provoking from a Persian general the exclamation: "How can we fight men like these who compete, not for material gains, but only for honor?"

All those who took part in the games were sacrosanct. From the heralds they received the formal blessing of the gods and a share of divinity. All were holy who attended the games.

About a month before the feast the competitors arrived at Elis, where they were carefully scrutinized. They had to prove they were Greeks and had committed no crimes, had been properly trained and would abide by the rulings of the officials. They swore on slices of boars' flesh that they would not sin against the Olympic games.

On the first day occurred the great sacrifices to Olympian Zeus. The white oxen were led before the double-tiered altar of Zeus, where they were sacrificed. The thighs were lifted onto the upper tier and burned; for the strength of the oxen was believed to be in the thighs,

which were especially favored by Zeus. On other altars were placed
offerings of honey cakes.

The first race was the chariot race in the hippodrome beginning
with a grand procession led by the marshals. It was a nine-mile course,
with altogether twenty-three turns around the statue of a horse
rearing on its hind legs. Sometimes forty four-horsed chariots took
part in the race. Alcibiades introduced seven teams of horses in one
race, winning first, second and fourth places; and he never permitted
the Athenians to forget that he had brought great honor on his city.
"Many have envied me, for did I not do everything in a style worthy
of my victory?" he said; and it was no more than the bitter truth.
Chariot racing was for the rich, and the gilded princes of Syracuse
were great contenders for the prize, not always successfully, for
when Dionysius of Syracuse entered the race, his chariot was deliberately upset by those who hated his tyranny.

The chariot races were in the morning. In the afternoon came the
Pentathlon, a combined contest of running, long jumping, discus and
javelin throwing, and wrestling. In the evening, under the golden
moon, the victors marched in procession and sang triumphal hymns.

The morning of the third day was spent in renewed sacrifices to
Zeus, but the games were resumed with the boys' competitions in
the afternoon. These boys were usually youths between seventeen
and twenty; sometimes they were younger, for the rules changed over
the centuries. They ran foot races, wrestled and boxed with the
cestus; and it was said that after these matches the boxers' dogs could
hardly recognize them. But if boxing was bad, the Pancration which
took place on the fourth day was worse. It was unarmed combat
of the most ferocious kind, with arm-twisting, eye-gouging and
kicking all permitted. It sometimes ended in death, and when a certain
Arrhicion of Phygalia died at the moment of victory, he was awarded
the crown.

The competitors sometimes went mad under the strain of the
games. Pausanias tells a wonderfully ghostly story about Cleomedes
of Astypalaia who killed Iccus of Epidaurus during a boxing match,
and went mad with grief and rage. He returned to his own town
and pulled down the pillars supporting the roof of a school, burying

sixty children under the debris. The terrified townsfolk pursued him with showers of stones. To escape them, he took sanctuary in the temple of Athene and jumped into a chest, holding down the lid with so much force that none could open it. When they brought up axes and hackled the chest open, Cleomedes had vanished. The oracle at Delphi told the townsfolk to worship him as "the last of the heroes."

On the last day there was the distribution of prizes, those slender olive wreaths which permitted the wearers to regard themselves as children of Zeus. Some received more permanent rewards. An Olympian victor from Athens could claim free board at the official guest house for the rest of his life; and when Socrates was put on trial and asked what punishment he deserved, he answered that he deserved the same honors which were given to Olympian victors. Sometimes the happy citizens would welcome a victor by tearing down part of the city wall, exclaiming that no one would dare to attack a city which possessed such a brave man. Spartans who won victories at the Olympian games were automatically enrolled in the King's bodyguard.

Pausanias, who visited Olympia in A.D. 174, relished the stories he learned about the athletes. Few are humorous; most are tragic, or tinged with tragedy. There is the story of the aging athlete Timanthes of Celonae, who discovered to his horror that he could no longer wield the bow he had been accustomed to bend every day. In remorse and horror of old age he built a funeral pyre and flung himself onto it. The most revealing of the stories describes how the two victorious sons of Diagoras, himself a victor in his day, carried their old father on their shoulders through the crowd. They were pelted with flowers. Then a voice came from the crowd, saying: "Die, Diagoras! There is nothing left to live for!" A moment later Diagoras was dead.

There were minor changes over the centuries. We hear that in the early days the runners were clothed, but in 720 B.C. Orsippus of Megara dropped his girdle in the foot race, and afterward the runners ran naked. Trainers, too, were forced to appear naked after Phereniké of Rhodes came disguised as her husband's trainer; her identity was discovered when she kissed him after his victory. Complete nakedness was demanded: not even a handkerchief might be used by the competitors to wipe the sweat away. All the races took part in the broiling heat of high summer.

When Nero came to Olympia, he observed all the rules scrupulously. It was very hot, but he refused to use a handkerchief to wipe the sweat away; instead he used the back of his arm. Like all the other competitors he spoke most deferentially to the judges, and in their presence he did not clear his throat or make any of the alarming noises he usually made when confronted by judges in contests. He drove a ten-horse chariot in Olympia, following the example of King Mithridates. He was thrown from it, picked up, put on the chariot again, but failed to stay the course. The judges wearily granted him the victory.

To the very end the Olympic contests were reserved for athletes, but at the beginning of the fourth century a special law was passed permitting competitions of heralds and trumpeters, who enjoyed a special place of honor in the games. Nero took part in the contests of the heralds, and won. Against all established custom he introduced competitions in singing and playing on the lyre. While he sang, no one was permitted to leave, with the result that men feigned death in order to escape. Nero was in such awe of the judges that he granted them all Roman citizenship and gave them vast sums of money. On the last day of the contests he was so enraged at the thought that others had won victories before him that he ordered the statues of victors to be thrown down and hurled into the latrines. Then there was only the spectacle of the triumphant Nero, *victor solus*, wearing on his head the olive crown of Olympia and carrying on his arm the crown of laurels from Delphi, since it was not permitted to wear two crowns at once.

Nero's visitation at Olympia was soon forgotten. The statues were hauled out of the latrines and set up within the sacred enclosure; and the judges solemnly announced that the Olympic games held under the auspices of Nero were removed from the sacred list of games.

Strangely, there was very little decline in the standard of the games during the centuries. The philosopher Xenophanes wondered aloud why athletes should be rewarded over philosophers; the athlete, he said, does not fill "the secret treasuries of the city with wealth." The citizens thought otherwise. They believed that the victor of the Pentathlon was almost superhuman and brought divinity to his city. Xenophanes was a very down-to-earth philosopher—he maintained that all things are derived from earth and water—and objected strongly to the introduction of divinity in what seemed to him to be a very mercenary competition. Xenophanes however was the exception. With varying degrees of belief the Greeks over a period of a thousand years continued to accept the festival of Olympia as an act of solemn annunciation and self-assertion in the presence of the gods. For them the holy truce, the sacrifices, the crowds, the steaming heat, the archaic heralds, the wise and bearded judges, the great temples, the sight of gleaming young bodies on the race track and the strangely gentle landscape of Olympia all combined to produce a quite extraordinary sense of harmony. In Olympia they found themselves.

No one spoke with greater authority about the games than Pindar. For him Olympia shone in the light of all the gods, but especially in the light of Apollo. In the "Sixth Olympian," a hymn in commemoration of the victory of Agesias of Syracuse, who was descended from Iamos, the child of Apollo and Evadne, Pindar even introduces a strange story of a holy baptism in the waters of the Alpheus:

> *The five-day child*
> *Lay in the long grasses and thickets, his tender body*
> *Heaped with the blue and yellow of the field-flowers,*
> *And therefore his mother gave him his immortal name,*
> *Iamos. In time the boy came*
> *Into his golden-helmeted youth, acquiring*
> *A ripe bloom. In his youth he waded*
> *Into the waters of the Alpheus, into midstream,*
> *Crying in a loud voice for his great forefather,*
> *Poseidon, and to his father Apollo,*
> *The Archer who dwelt in heavenly built Delos,*
> *In the darkness of the night, praying*
> *For the crown of honor and the love of the people.*

Then from close at hand there came his father's voice,
Saying: "Arise, my son, follow my voice,
Come to the place of welcoming!" So they climbed
Together the sheer rock of towering Kronios,
And the god placed in his hands the gift of prophecy,
The power to command. . . .

Iamos was the founder of the princely family of hereditary sooth-sayers of Olympia, but "the gift of prophecy, the power to command" were believed to accompany all victors in the games. Victory in the games placed a seal on the athletes; and as the Middle Ages canonized the ascetic saints, the Greeks canonized their athletes. There were excellent psychological reasons why these athletes might be supposed to possess qualities absent in lesser mortals: they were touched with the calm of the gods. So Pindar described them as "conquerors who keep through all their years a honeyed calm, the fruit of their high deeds. Nothing is loftier than this nobility which clothes each common day."

The Olympic games might have gone on forever, if Christianity had not asserted itself in opposition to the celebration of handsome youths. When the Emperor Theodosius II gave the order for the destruction of the temple of Zeus in A.D. 426, the last games had already been held. They had long since outlived their usefulness. There were too many heroes to be commemorated; there were too many statues, too many priests, too many temples, too many sacrifices. In the end the Olympic games perished, not because they were outlawed by a Christian Emperor, but because they were suffocated by the weight of the past. Yet never in the history of human institutions had a tradition lasted for so long.

To the very end the records of the games were kept with scrupulous accuracy. Ironically, the last recorded victor was a Persian, Varazdates, belonging to the race of the hereditary enemies of Greece. He won the boxing match in A.D. 385.

In time Olympia was sacked by the Goths under Alaric, and a succession of earthquakes leveled the temples. By A.D. 551 hardly one stone was standing on another. Twice the river Kladeos altered its course and flowed over the ruins, drowning the sanctuary in sand

and pebbles. A Byzantine church was built on the site where once stood the temple of Zeus. In the last years of the Middle Ages, Olympia became a quarry, even its name forgotten. In the sixteenth century the place was known as Andilalo. The shepherds wandered about the fields, and they did not know that under their feet lay the altars of the gods, and some of the greatest sculptures ever made.

THE FACE OF ZEUS

When the German archaeologists came to Olympia and dug through an entire village, and then through sand and clay until they had uncovered the sanctuary of Olympia, there was one object they hoped to discover above any others—the great statue of Zeus enthroned, made of gold and ivory, towering forty feet high, so majestic that everyone who saw it caught his breath, and some wondered whether it was not Zeus himself. It was the crowning achievement of Phidias, and one of the wonders of the world.

The German archaeologists never found the statue, but they uncovered the grey stone pedestal on which he once sat enthroned, the pediments of his temple and a small figure of Victory which stood in the vestibule of the temple. Most of their important work was finished by 1881. Some seventy-five years later, in 1956, they found not far from the temple the molds in which the gold drapery of Zeus had been hammered into place. These molds were of terra cotta, the larger pieces braced with iron, and they learned that the gold was inlaid with glass. Nothing else, not even a single ivory finger, has come to light.

Among the ancients there was universal agreement that the statue possessed extraordinary beauty and majesty. The Roman general Aemilius Paulus came to Olympia after conquering Greece, gazed at the statue and declared that he was moved "as by the very presence of the God." Cicero declared that it could not have been made after any living model, but had been fashioned on an ideal image. Quintilian said the majesty of the statue equaled the majesty of the God—*adeo majestis operis deum aequavit.* Dio Chrysostom called it "the most beautiful image on earth, and the dearest to the gods," and went on to declare, in a famous oration which reads like a prayer: "Let one who has drained the cup of sorrows and from whom sleep is banished stand before this statue, and he will forget all the griefs and troubles which encumber the paths of men."

It was, then, a statue of remarkable majesty and power, of an almost unearthly dignity and composure, representing the Greek ideal of divinity in the portrait of the most powerful of the gods.

There is a legend that when Panaenos, the brother of Phidias, asked him how he would represent Zeus, Phidias replied with three lines of Homer:

> *Zeus spoke and with thundering brows nodded assent,*
> *While his ambrosial hair on his immortal head*
> *Waved forward; and Olympus quaked with terror.*

Yet from all accounts of the statue there was only a faint hint of terror. Calm, majesty, a brooding benevolence, a certain austerity, all these were contained in the statue which was richly draped in gold plate and surrounded by a vast quantity of jeweled and sculptured ornaments. Above all there was a sense of ripeness, of a maturity almost beyond any imaginable maturity. Power streamed from the forty-foot-high statue of Zeus. There was vigor and even youthfulness in the body, but the face was old with the wisdom of the ages.

Pausanias, who took careful notes when he visited the sanctuary, provides an exhaustive catalogue of all the decorations to the throne. There is something forbidding in the vast profusion of ivory statues, painted friezes, inlays and decorative figures embellishing it.

The artist seems to have felt a compulsion to fill up all the available space with designs, which reared up from the chair rests, the cross bars and the back of the throne. Along the edge of the seat, just above eye level, was depicted Apollo's merciless destruction of the children of Niobe. The wars between the Greeks and the Amazons were depicted along the cross bars. Nine panels of paintings covered the screens which enclosed the entire lower part of the throne, with the heroes and the gods depicted in their moments of triumph or disaster. Prometheus bound was shown; so were Theseus and Peirithoös, and Hellas and Salamis, Ajax and Cassandra, and the dying Penthesilea. Hercules was represented on all three sides of the panel. On the footstool flanked with golden lions Theseus fought against the Amazons, and on the pedestal supporting the throne Aphrodite rose from the waves into the arms of Eros and Peitho. The legs of the throne were golden Victories; the arms were Sphinxes; the uprights at the back of the throne were dominated by the hovering forms of the Graces and the Hours. A confused and repetitive ornamentation overlaid the throne.

There was nothing, however, confused in the statue of Zeus seated in stern splendor on a golden throne set with precious stones, one hand bearing the gold and ivory figure of Victory, the other holding a scepter inlaid with precious metals and surmounted by a golden eagle. The chest was bare. A gold mantle enveloped his legs and all the lower part of his body, and hung in folds from his left shoulder. Face, chest, shoulders and arms were all of ivory, and were painted. His sandals were gold. Below lay a floor of black tiles with a ring of Parian marble to retain the olive oil which was continually being poured over the statue to keep the ivory fresh; and the god was seen in the diffused and shimmering light thrown up by the sunlight falling on the bath of oil.

Pausanias says nothing about his features, but there were coins minted in Elis during classical times which enable us to put together piece by piece the details of his face. There are two coins, one showing the head in profile, the other showing him on the throne. He has deepset eyes, a low forehead, a long straight nose, a heavy mustache which curls over the edges of the mouth, and a thick beard neatly trimmed. The lips are parted, as though he were about to speak. He wears the wreath of olive leaves, the victor's prize at Olympia.

The face in its power and beauty resembles a little the stern Pantocrator at Daphni. If the coins can be trusted, the upper part of the face is astonishingly young. Remove the beard, and there is a man of about thirty, very grave, meditative, heavy with responsibility. There is even a hint of femininity in the long curling strands of hair, seven or eight separate rivers of hair, which fall over his shoulder. He has small ears and a powerful neck, and the hair on the crown of his head is combed forward in careful waves. There is, in that face, the faintest suggestion of the Orient, of some distant Ionian origin, perhaps even some memory of the bearded kings of Persia.

Many influences have worked upon that face. There is nothing in the least simple about it. But all these influences have fused together to form the features of a beneficent, all-powerful and terrible divinity. To our astonishment we recognize the face of Christ.

Perhaps it is something we should have suspected from the beginning. The ancient ceremony never came entirely to an end. The features which were worshiped in the fifth century B.C. were to be worshiped through all the remaining years of the civilization which had its origin in Greece as much as in Palestine. Olympian Zeus, shattered by earthquakes or removed by a Christian Emperor to decorate a street in Byzantium, haunts us still, as he haunted the Greeks who gazed up at him in fear and trembling, and with almost intolerable joy. Through those half-open lips spoke the unheard voice of God.

Suetonius tells the story of the mad Emperor Caligula giving orders shortly before his death for the statue to be broken into pieces and removed to Rome. The workmen set up their scaffolding, when suddenly a great peal of laughter was heard. The scaffolding collapsed and the workmen took to their heels. It is not a story we need believe, but it is important that it was believed in the time of Suetonius. To the Romans of the first century A.D. the Zeus of Olympia was still the greatest of all the gods.

Even in our own time, though nothing remains of the statue except the evidence of the coins and the terra-cotta molds of his garment, the Zeus of Phidias still rules over men. In countless paintings and statues in countless churches the familiar face can be seen, eternally young and eternally old, eternally warning and eternally blessing. "He is the god of peace," said Dio Chrysostom, "supremely gentle, dispenser of being and life and all good things, the father and saviour and guardian of men."

On one of the pine-scented slopes overlooking the Kladeos and the sanctuary stands a small museum not much larger than a cattle shed. It holds the most impressive collection of Greek sculptures in the world, and the greatest of these stand along a single wall.

There was a time when the pediments of Olympia were regarded with some distaste. They were thought to be heavy and unfinished, and it was pointed out that the draperies were sculptured without delicacy. "Is there a single figure on either of these pediments that deserves to be called beautiful?" asked Frazer. The pediments were dismissed, and praise was reserved for the Hermes of Praxiteles, a headless statue of Victory from the porch of the temple of Zeus, and a vast quantity of coins and inscriptions found during the excavations.

The Hermes of Praxiteles still holds the place of honor. He stands in an alcove above a sandbath in case he should topple over during an earthquake: the only statue at Olympia to be so protected. Special lighting has been arranged, his missing legs have been restored, and visitors are not allowed to approach him. Pausanias saw the statue during his visit to Olympia and noted among the offerings dedicated to the temple of Hera "a Hermes of marble with the infant Dionysus, by Praxiteles." The statue was found near the temple of Hera in 1877, and there seems to be no doubt that this is an original work by Praxiteles.

He stands there in all his languorous beauty, the milk-white flesh so delicate that one imagines that if one touched it with a thumb, the thumb print would remain. Cupped on his left arm is a wizened child, but Hermes is paying no attention to him; he is gazing vacantly, and a little sorrowfully, into the distance. The child is reaching for something, or perhaps waving his hand for attention. The sculptor has only sketched in the marble hair which rises in curious lumps as though covered with soapsuds. There is a fleshy protuberance on the forehead, and the eyes have been sketched in lightly, with the effect of a kind of chiaroscuro, giving him his famous blank look. There is a short upper lip, but the mouth is voluptuously feminine; he has a small chin and a nose as sharp as a pen. Only the thighs and the testicles have an abundant life, and they seem to belong to another figure entirely. Remove the head, the upraised stump of the arm and the incoherent child, and we would have a torso of superb and disquieting delicacy. It is the torso of a very young and effeminate man, with an uncanny resemblance to a Botticelli St. Sebastian.

To the ancient Greeks, Hermes was the fastest runner among the gods, the protector of travelers, the god of prudence and cunning, perjury and theft. It is odd that he should be represented as a youth of such dewy-eyed effeminacy.

The Victory of Paeonios is a far more distinguished work, but the museum curators have thought fit to attach to it a crumbled head with no recognizable features. No doubt the head belongs to the body, but no doubt also it is an affront to the exquisitely delicate girl who has just flown down from heaven. Beneath her feet there can be made out the head of the eagle of Zeus, who accompanied her on her journey.

The poor smashed head gives an almost surrealist effect to the Victory: the same effect might be achieved by cutting off the head of the Venus de Milo and substituting a football.

This angelic messenger from the heavens wears only the lightest of garments, and as she descends to the earth, plummeting down from the throne of God, her transparent veils are visibly pressed against her young body. The sculptor has caught the moment just before impact, before she touches the earth, and before the inevitable jolt. Headless, armless, without wings, she forms almost an abstract portrait of "an angel alighting," a thing of cloudy forms and milk-white ripples, of tag ends of cloth caught up by a breast or flung sideways by the wind. Those tempestuous folds are frozen in an instantaneous moment, and have something in common with those instantaneous photographs showing a bullet in flight or an expanding soap bubble. There are folds of all kinds: the gentle, only barely discernible folds on her left thigh, the heavy ridged folds falling from the covered breast, and the tremendous explosive folds which, around the waist, whip like banners in a high wind.

Records survive, showing how this Victory once stood in the porch of the temple of Zeus on a high triangular base. An inscription records that it was dedicated by the Messenians and Naupactians from the spoils of their victory over the Spartans in 424 B.C. There was once an inscription on the base, reading: "For the victory of the Messenians over the Spartans." Quite naturally the Spartans raised objections, pointing out that they were the only nation to receive such treatment at the temple of Zeus, and the Messenians obligingly changed the inscription to read: "For the victory of the Messenians over their enemies." According to the Messenians everyone knew they had only one enemy—the Spartans.

The Victory we see today is very young, not at all assured of herself, only tentatively touching the earth, and self-consciously aware of the astonishing beauty of her body, which is not yet completely formed. She is deliciously virginal and dovelike, unlike the Victory of Samothrace, who is a woman of imposing maturity. Time has dealt kindly with the young Victory, destroying all that is ephemeral and inconsequential, while preserving all that is graceful, nervous and childlike.

It is a pity she is stuck limply against a wall, with no special lighting to indicate the freshness and brilliance of her youth, for she is an incomparably greater work than the Hermes of Praxiteles. This divine messenger has the breath of life in her; she belongs to the air and sunlight; and her divinity is completely convincing.

But the museum has even greater things than the Victory. It has sculptures of such staggering greatness and majesty that one wonders how they could ever have been allowed to fall into the earth, and once excavated, how they could ever fail to be regarded as among the very greatest works ever conceived. These sculptures from the western pediment of the temple of Zeus are badly lit and atrociously displayed, and most of them are in a ruined condition, but they have a fire and energy and overwhelming beauty which have the effect of destroying all the other sculptures in the room. Here is perfection so absolute that it is disturbing.

A good deal is known about the sculptor Alcamenes, but except for a Roman copy of his statue of Ares, now in the Louvre, very little of his work apart from these sculptures on the west pediment can be identified. His famous Aphrodite of the Gardens is lost. Lucian writing in the second century amused himself by imagining an ideal Aphrodite, in which many sculptors had a hand. He imagined a forehead and eyes by Praxiteles, the contours of the face and the nostrils by Phidias, the smiling lips and draperies by Sosandra, "while the round of her cheek and the front of her face together with the hands and the beautiful flow of the wrists, and the delicately shaped tapering fingers shall follow the Aphrodite of the Gardens by Alcamenes." Lucian had studied sculpture, and it is evident that he regarded Alcamenes as the master of the fluent line and the delicate carving of muscles. It is possible that Alcamenes sculpted the Caryatids of the Erechtheion: they are abundantly in his style. The story is told that Phidias and Alcamenes were commissioned to make two statues of Athene to be set up on lofty columns. When seen on the ground the Athene of Alcamenes appeared to be the far superior work, but when it was elevated it was seen to be inferior, for Phidias knew more about perspective. In his lifetime Alcamenes was praised for his delicacy rather than for his sense of robust splendor. But it is the marriage of delicacy and splendor which appears on the west pediment.

The sculptures portray the combat between the Lapiths and the Centaurs at the wedding of Peirithoös, prince of the Lapiths. The wedding guests included Theseus, King of Athens, and Caeneus, a Lapith youth who had once been a girl and was changed by the gods and made immortal. Hippodamia, the daughter of the king of Elis, was the bride, and the leader of the enraged and drunken Centaurs was Eurytion.

Pausanias, who saw the sculpture when it stood some fifty feet high above the ground, described it at some length and so accurately that we can make out each of the personages he mentions:

> At the center of the pediment is Peirithoös. On one side of him is Eurytion, who had seized the wife of Peirithoös, and Caeneus is bringing help to him, and on the other side is Theseus defending himself against the Centaurs with an ax. One Centaur has seized a maiden, another a boy in the prime of life. I believe Alcamenes carved this scene because he had learned from Homer's poem that Peirithoös was a son of Zeus.

All this is definite enough, and there is no reason to suppose that Pausanias was misled by the guides. Some modern scholars are inclined to believe that since Zeus was represented in the central position on the eastern pediment, only one of the greatest of the gods could be represented in a similar position on the western pediment. Accordingly the central figure is usually described as Apollo, and it is assumed that Pausanias was regretfully credulous or absent-minded.

One would like to believe it is Apollo. That majestic figure, who rises so superbly above the conflict, indicating his overwhelming power over the combatants with a gesture of imperious authority, so calm, so pitiless, so supremely confident in his physical beauty—how, we ask, can this be one of the lesser gods? Pausanias supplies the excellent answer. "I believe Alcamenes carved this scene because he had learned from Homer's poem that Peirithoös was the son of Zeus."

This statue so dominates the pediment that it is a long time before the eyes can register the supremely effective design of the whole. That sovereign gesture controls the entire scene, knits it together, sends wave upon wave of energy flowing backwards and forwards through it. We are the witnesses of a drama of suspended action, a pause in a solemn rite, the sacred performance of an ancient play. The participants themselves become mysterious spectators of the scene they are enacting: there is the sense that everything is *known*. The Centaurs know they will be crushed; the captured women know that they will leap out of the embrace; the slaves who crouch in the far corners peer up like children at the bestial fury of the Centaurs, hardly believing it is taking place. They are the observers of the battle. For the first time instead of river gods or the heads of horses the sloping corners of the pediments contain the audience.

Nothing so self-conscious as this pediment was ever constructed in Greece except the Parthenon itself; but there are no sculptures on the Parthenon to match these. The world of Alcamenes is cool, composed, lucid, never agitated or sentimental; he never overstates. He achieves nobility without pretentiousness, and in the figure of Peirithoös he achieves majesty.

The young god wears his hair like a helmet, and at one time must have worn a gold crown, for there are rivet holes behind his ears. His mantle was once red—traces of red paint still remain on it. He may have held a spear in his outflung hand, and he almost certainly held a sword in the other: once again time has been merciful, destroying all that was inessential. One leg has been broken off at the knee, and there are no feet, but that is not too great a loss, for everything else remains and much of the surface seems as fresh as when it left the sculptor's studio. It is a figure stamped with archaism, without the excessive refinement of the figures on the Parthenon frieze, with no curling and curving draperies, no soft modeling of the torso, and except in the hair no intricate designs.

But it is the face of the young god, modeled with a calm and luminous severity, which shows the sculptor at his best. The hair comes so low that it conceals the forehead, the eyes are wide open and heavily lidded under the enormous sweep of the brows, and the rounded chin is unusually heavy and powerful. The lips are full and sensual, suggesting Asia rather than Greece. The face expresses at once the plenitude of power and of experience.

So it is with the faces of the Lapith women, who all bear a family resemblance to Peirithoös. They have the same untroubled gaze, the same unclouded fullness of cheeks and chin, the same expressions of calm authority. The hands of a Centaur tear at the breast of Hippodamia, but she shows no alarm. She is in the conflict, but not of it; she knows that the Centaurs are doomed, and that the spectacle, in which she is quietly absorbed, will soon be over. The arm of a young Lapith warrior is being bitten by a Centaur, and he too shows only the faintest alarm. Yet throughout the pediment there is the sense of violent movement, an outbreak of bestial fury about to be calmed. No one ever suggested so well the calm of the gods.

In the paintings of Mantegna there is sometimes to be found the figure of a dreaming youth leaning on his spear in the midst of wild battle. He too is apart from the conflict, while somehow dominating it, for he exerts his sovereignty over his dreams, and the whole painting can be conceived as a dream emanating from him. So, too, with the west pediment at Olympia we are made aware of dreamlike ges-

tures, of an entire landscape of dreams, of a bestiality so terrible that it can only be hinted at, and of a nobility and majesty so great that they can only be imagined in dreams. And yet in some mysterious way Alcamenes has turned the dream into living stone.

The triumph of Alcamenes is that he was the first to depict the European intelligence, and he accomplished this in a figure of grave majesty. His Peirithoös is a man who conquers by intelligence alone. He is recognizably human, while remaining a god. He is no Prometheus, who has stormed heaven, for he belongs to heaven. That gesture of authority comes easily to him; and his hidden brows are wild with imagination. He stands on that pinnacle where, for a brief while, the Greeks were able to see the world around them with pitiless lucidity, everything arranged in order under the calm sun. From those loins sprang science, and from that gesture came authority over all the things of the earth.

Only once again, among the surviving Greek sculptures, can we observe a beauty approaching this. There is in Athens a bronze of a bearded hero with his arms outflung, fashioned perhaps by Phidias, which equals it in authority, but not in grace, nor in knowledge, nor in self-conscious pride. To Peirithoös alone was it given to see the flower opening. On that dreaming face can be seen all the dangerous intelligence which came to birth in the West. He is the architect who designed our skyscrapers, the mechanic who first sent airplanes into the air, the builder of ships, the superb navigator. He stands at the beginning of European history; and we might have guessed that he would wear the indelible marks of tragedy.

His spear, his sword, his jeweled crown are lost; he stands before us in unselfconscious nakedness like a young king dreaming his life away, and there is on his face such sweetness and serenity that we may well assume he will never harm anything on earth. Then look again, and you will see he is merciless.

I had spent the day in Olympia wandering among the ruins, and from time to time returning to the museum to see whether Peirithoös was still there, as beautiful as I had imagined, and then it was evening. In the thick shadows, under the pines, the ruins assume the shape of boulders left by the last ice age. All order is lost. One temple merges into another. At that hour the only sound comes from the shepherds playing their pipes in the hills.

It was not quite dark when I saw the cave. It was a very small cave, perhaps an inch long, under a twisted olive tree, near the great white boulders which are all that remains of the temple of Hera. In that eerie light I saw the ants making their way to the cave, hundreds of them, and all of them were carrying husks of wheat, for there is always some wheat scattered among the temples: the peasants in the neighborhood use the vast monolithic platform of the temple of Zeus as a threshing floor.

So they came, like an army, in long thin lines, making their way over pebbles and seashell-encrusted stones, and they were nearly invisible under their loads of wheat, which waved crazily in the wind. They formed yellow columns, and sometimes there were stragglers who wandered off the main roads, and were lost, but there were not many of these.

I remember they had difficulty entering the cave, which was high up on the side of a small three-inch cliff, and rubble kept falling over the entrance. So the ants would stop and allow their burdens to tumble to the ground, and then they would attack the mouth of the cave until it was large enough to let them in. They worked calmly. They seemed to know exactly what to do at every moment, and except for the stragglers they never hesitated.

What was frightening, in that time and that place, was the element of ceremony. It was easy to forget that they were simply storing the husks. They seemed to be coming to some sacred place, bringing offerings, as for century upon century the Greeks brought offerings to Olympia. Those yellow husks in the fading light gleamed like gold. There were some ants larger than the others, resembling horsemen, and they carried the heaviest loads. There were small husks and large husks, husks like chariots, husks like boats. From all over the sanctuary they came in unwavering lines with offerings for the goddess of the cave.

I was watching them as Zeus must have watched from Olympus the sacrifices which took place here. I was so far away from them that they paid no attention to me. They were safe in the darkness; safe too in the knowledge that they were performing the proper rites, with great difficulty, according to prescribed rules. They poured into the darkness of the cave and were swallowed up.

There all round me were the little bobbing golden husks amid the silvery gleam of the seashells, and the pine-scented wind was coming over the hills. I do not know what came over me. I remember kicking brutally at the mouth of the cave and scattering them in confusion. Then for a while I felt I had committed a greater crime than Theodosius II when he destroyed the temples.

V DELOS

Mycenae has the heaviness of dread, and Olympia is heavy with the weight of years. They belong to the Peloponnese, to the dark shadowed coasts, the craggy mountains and the haunted valleys. It was not from them that there came the shining in the air, or the singing of the youthful gods.

There came a time perhaps in the ninth century B.C. when rumors of a young and handsome god armed with a bow of gold reached the mainland of Greece. He was a god who combined exquisite grace with a sense of quiet ruthlessness. He had been a sun god and wore the spiked crown of the sun, but in some mysterious, barely discernible way he had stepped down from his chariot to move among men, while remaining in the heavens. He announced the new law that the earth belonged to the creators of music and poetry. He was no muscle-bound Hercules straining after victories of the flesh; his victories were those of the sunlit mind, and the contemplative spirit.

We shall never know how he came to earth, or why he settled on the island of Delos and consecrated it by his presence. He seems to have had his origin in Lycia, but his entire history before the goddess Leto gave birth to him on Delos remains unknown. He had been born before, and may be born again. He was "the far-shining one," "the friend of Zeus," "the giver of music and song." Nothing the Greeks ever created was so magnificent as this youth who tore the darkness from the human soul and let in the human light.

The landscapes tell the story. Just as the heroic age in Greece reflects the mountains of the Argolid, and the beneficence of Zeus is expressed in the rolling hills of Olympia, so Delos describes a portrait of Apollo. Even today the holy island expresses the abstract image of the god.

There are white islands all round Delos, all shining and a little ghostly. The Greeks spoke of those islands as the Cyclades, "the wheeling ones," and they still seem to wheel around the small and mysterious island which stands so lonely in their midst.

It lies very low on the water with only the small hill of Cynthus to hold it from floating away. The blue and violet seas wash its shores, and the winds are fresh and sweet. In spring it is a mass of flowers, whole sheets of anemones flooding the meadows filled with gleaming columns and ruins glittering like bones. In summer it is parched, with thistles and barley grass growing thick among the ruins, and in winter the winds of the Aegean pour over it, smoothing out the folds of the draperies of the few remaining statues.

One should come to Delos on one of those transparent-blue mornings when the sea is very still and the *meltemi* is blowing softly. One should come leisurely in one of the black boats belonging to the Naxian fishermen, whose skins have turned to leather. Their wives are waiting. They will try to sell you embroideries and dyed stuffs, telling you it is all made in the Cyclades, though it comes from Athens, as soon as the boat has pushed its way over the shelving pebbles and the waving reeds. The wives will not complain overmuch if you buy nothing. What is astonishing is that once you have landed and the whole island stretches before you, you become aware of an enchantment of formidable proportions.

The virgin island, where no one was allowed to be born or to die or to fall sick, remains virgin still, and a divine light falls over it. At first there is an effect of strangeness, even of unreality; and this sense of unreality continues as you become aware of the light from all the other islands continually beating down on Delos, the flood of light in which Delos seems to succumb; and the whole air is full of the reverberations of light, white marble flashing against white marble. Over Delos the air is a dancing quivering flame, and all the islands around are like mirrors giving shape to the light, to the great blue dome of the Apollonian heaven.

Delos, then, is this light, this strange glitter and shining high up in the air, a mysterious quivering, the beating of silver wings. There is this very rich, very pure light, never still, and when the eyes have grown accustomed to it, then at last the island loses its fragility, as a golden chalice seen through curtains and lit by flickering candles also loses its fragility after a while as the eyes grow accustomed to it.

One must begin with the light, for the god of light was born here and the Greeks were perfectly aware of the strange quality of light which bathes the island. They recognized the shimmering presence of the god in the air above, and they set about making the island worthy of him; and this was made all the easier because the island is very small and low—three miles long, a mile wide, and the highest hill no more than 350 feet high.

In the beginning, according to the *Homeric Hymn to Delian Apollo*, the island was very dubious about whether it could support the presence of the god:

> *How shall I receive the god, the proud one,*
> *The arrogant one who stands in the highest place*
> *Above all the gods and people of the teeming earth?*
> *My heart is fearful at the thought of his coming,*
> *For when he sees me at the first leap of the sunrise*
> *Surely he will despise me, a heap of barren stones!*
> *He will press his foot on me, he will thrust me*
> *Into the depths of the sea, and the waves will wash over me,*
> *And then he will turn away into another place*
> *And build his temples in a land of fruitful trees,*
> *And I shall be lost in the dark sea. Only the black seals*
> *And the octopuses shall live on me. . . .*

As we know, the island was wrong. Instead of black seals and octopuses there came the most beautiful of the gods and a myriad temples, and all the wealth of Greece poured into the island treasury. Apollo not only came to the island, but chose to be born on it, and the Greeks never tired of celebrating his birth. Theognis in the sixth century

B.C. spoke of how the goddess Leto "grasped the palm tree in her tender hands and gave birth to the fairest of the immortals beside the wheel-shaped lake, and the whole earth laughed for joy," and three centuries later Callimachus described how the island blazed in a golden glory at the moment of birth:

> *Gold were the foundations of the island,*
> *Gold were the ripples in the wheel-shaped lake,*
> *Gold was the sheltering palm tree,*
> *Gold were the rolling floods of the river Inopus,*
> *And gold was the ground from which the Mother lifted up her Son.*

They said that to celebrate his birth the islands of the Cyclades wheeled round in holy joy, and strange perfumes were wafted over the island, and white swans suddenly appeared on the lake. Leto did not give her son milk from her breast: she gave him ambrosia and nectar, and he grew up tall and straight in the twinkling of an eye. For centuries a palm tree marked the place where he was born, and Odysseus remembered the fresh beauty of the palm tree beside the lake when he emerged from the reeds and saw Nausicaä playing ball with her maids. "I never saw anyone so beautiful, neither man nor woman," he declared. "I am blinded by admiration, and I can only compare you with the young palm tree which I saw when I was at Delos growing near the altar of Apollo."

Apollo had found his home, and he ruled the world from Delos. He conquered by the power of his beauty; he had no earthly resources, no armies, no navies, no powerful government. In the beginning his sole possession was a barren island.

Today the island is barren again, and crowded with ruins. There is hardly a square inch of the island which does not lie under the shadow of some broken columns, or a broken wall. The only inhabitants are the grey speckled lizards which shelter underneath the stones, and the yellow butterflies dancing among the columns. Even now no one lives on the island.

Two hundred years ago, when Alexander Drummond made his famous journey from Scotland through all Europe and the Near East, he remarked on the strange sense of loss which comes to nearly all visitors as they wander among the ruins. "When we landed on Delos," he wrote, "mine eyes were struck with the immense quantity of broken marble, and my heart was pierced with real concern to see the devastations which have been made among such glorious edifices, and which I considered as the ruins of some friend's habitation. I therefore walked on with a kind of sullen pensiveness."

It is difficult to avoid that "sullen pensiveness." The ruins of Olympia are mute; the great columns are flaking away, becoming once more the seashells out of which they were formed; there is no feeling of a continuing festival. But as you walk through the barley grass at Delos, among the ruins of Parian marble which glitter with a grave purity, very pure, very white, there is always the impression that the festival has been mysteriously interrupted by some unimaginable catastrophe—not war, not time, nothing that can be apprehended by the mind—and very soon, and in some quite unpredictable way, it will be resumed. The stones are only waiting to rise again.

Wandering among the ruins, you become aware of an expectant quietness, the presence of an unexplained mystery which will shortly be revealed. There is a strange lull. The island is under a spell. The coastline is fretted with lace, and everywhere you look there are white islands. Soon Prospero will descend from his mountain cave and with his wand bring the island back to life again.

It is one of those islands where Shakespeare would have found himself at home, and indeed he remembered travelers' tales about Delos when he came to write *The Winter's Tale:*

CLEOMENES

The climate's delicate, the air most sweet;
Fertile the isle, the temple much surpassing
The common praise it bears.

DION

               I shall report,
For most it caught me, the celestial habits
(Methinks I so should term them) and the reverence
Of the grave wearers. O, the sacrifice!
How ceremonious, solemn, and unearthly
It was i' th' off'ring!

Not, of course, that Apollo was the sole god who ever lived on Delos. Long before Apollo 'leapt forth into the light of day,' there must have been temples in the hills where the gods were worshiped. No one any longer remembers who they were, or how they were worshiped; we know that they existed and that the radiance of Apollo was like an acetylene torch, burning them until almost no trace of them remained.

There are inexplicable gaps in the story of Apollo's visitation, and curious legends. The *Homeric Hymn to Delian Apollo* mentions that Leto was leaning against Mount Cynthus when she gave birth to Apollo, and at the same time she was grasping the sacred palm tree. We are told too that two great waves, coming from east and west, rose against the island at the moment of his birth. We hear of Apollo hunting the deer and offering their horns on the altar of Zeus after slaughtering every single beast in sight. The god of calm and sunlight could on occasion be wildly murderous, as when he slew all the children of Niobe because she had boasted of the fertility of her loins. Pindar preserves what is evidently a fragment of an old legend when he spoke of Apollo "smiling to see the rampant lust of the lewd beasts."

Evidently the clean-limbed god devoted to music and the arts derived from a more primitive god, who drew his strength from mountains and huge waves and murderous lusts. He was not always the god of the pure sunlight; he was the god who killed with heat stroke and with plague, and his golden arrow was dipped in poison. Huge and terrible he stalked the island, and he did not dwell beside the shore, but on the rocky slopes of Mount Cynthus on the further side of the island.

Cynthus is little more than a hillock, but so barren, so massive in comparison with everything else on the low-lying island that it gives an impression of rugged grandeur. Here, in a natural cleft in the rock, is a cave formed by five pairs of enormous slabs of grey granite, which are like nothing so much as the slabs forming the great passageway at Tiryns. Cyclopean stones led to the cave. In front there is a sacrificial pit and a marble base where a tripod may have stood. There are the remains of an altar.

It is a darkly ominous place, and quite the oldest of the innumerable sanctuaries on the island, belonging to a time long before Mycenae. The cave leads nowhere, but it suggests power, the menace of an ancient past, some crime committed once on the slopes. Tradition speaks of it as the original home of Apollo. Here offerings were made to him, and here worshipers came to listen to the prophecies of the priestess. Aeneas seems to have visited this cave during his wanderings, for Virgil describes how he came to the temple and marveled at the ancient stones piled high on one another, and how, after he had begged Apollo to guide him, "the hill seemed to quake, and the entrance to the sanctuary and the sacred bay tree were shaking, and the whole shrine seemed to be thrown wide open, and there came from the tripod a voice like thunder."

The voice told Aeneas to seek for "the ancient mother," and when he had settled in the kingdom which had been prophesied for him, then his descendants would rule over "the farthest limits of the earth." With that happy promise he sailed past the green Isle of Reeds and the Isle of Olives and marble-white Paros, and landed in Crete, where he built a city, and when the pestilences came and he saw his small band dying all round him he thought of returning to Delos and once more asking the advice of Apollo. But Apollo came to him in a dream and spoke of a land far to the west called Hesperia. So Aeneas abandoned Crete and sailed westward to Italy, obeying the god who lived in the cave.

Terror lurks in that shadowed cave. It is not a place where one would shelter from the heat. Like the grave circle of Mycenae it speaks of ancient murders and endless sacrifices and crimes committed by kings, not in passion but in their cold lusts. It is a fit place for a god of terror. What is strange is that it should be associated with the god of clarity and song.

Above the cave, on the summit of Cynthus, there is another altar of grey granite, now broken and crumbling. Cyclopean steps lead to it. Here once more we are in the presence of Apollo, the clear sky, the whole island at our feet, and as far as the eye can see lie the Cyclades, dancing like a chorus around the sacred island, all white and gleaming under the sun. Their shapes are youthful. Syros, Tinos, Myconos, Naxos and Paros form the inner ring, but there are others stretching to the horizon, and all of them sparkle with the same grave, pure light. To one of these islands came Danaë drifting in a chest, clutching the infant Perseus in her arms. Somewhere on Ios, one of the smaller islands, lies the grave of Homer.

ARCHAIC TORSO

There are two places on the island where suddenly you become aware of the power of the god. One of these places is the haunted cave on Cynthus. The other is near the ruined temple of Apollo close to the shore. At first sight it appears to be no more than a marble boulder, very white and dominating by its sheer bulk, but otherwise unremarkable. There are faint markings on it, but these, except for a row of delicate curls worn smooth by the weather, might have been formed by the accidents of time. It does not look like Apollo, but it is all that is left of the greatest statue of Apollo ever made.

At some time in the sixth century B.C. the people of the neighboring island of Naxos, grown rich from their ownership of silver mines and marble quarries, decided to make an offering to the god. It would be the largest, the most imposing, the most perfectly sculptured of all. They employed the sculptors Tektaeos and Angelion to carve an Apollo some thirty feet high, showing him standing naked and upright, his arms bent forward in the attitude of someone offering gifts, one hand holding a golden bow, the other holding a kind of golden plate bearing the images of the three Graces, Euphrosyne who commanded song, Thalia who commanded dancing, and Aglaia who commanded all that was bright and shining in the world. One of the Graces was playing on a lyre, another on a flute, a third on a shepherd's pipe. We do not have to seek far for an explanation of the presence of the Graces. According to Pindar they had set their thrones beside Apollo, for his kingdom was that of Grace.

This colossal statue together with its base was carved from a single block of Naxian marble and bore an archaic inscription: "Statue and foundation are one."

It had been standing for about a hundred and fifty years when in 418 B.C. the Greek general Nicias, the millionaire owner of silver mines in Attica, became appalled by the lack of decorum of the worshipers who flocked to the Temple of Apollo in Delos. He was determined to revive the proper rituals and display his own magnificence. He sailed to the island of Rheneia, and during the night he threw a gilded bridge hung with garlands and tapestries across the narrows. At dawn he led the procession to the temple. There were feasts, games and sacrifices, and he presented Apollo with an enormous bronze palm tree.

Never had there been so many sumptuously dressed choristers, so many precious gifts offered to the god. Quite deliberately Nicias had set himself the task of appeasing the god and reviving the ancient ceremonies, for only a few years before, in the time of Pericles, all the treasure of Delos had been removed to Athens to furnish the temples on the Acropolis; and when the Delians objected, Pericles said: "To what better use can the treasure be put?" The Athenians were obscurely aware they had committed a crime against Apollo, and Nicias was determined to bask in the god's favor.

He did more than offer prayers: he bought a few acres of ground near the temple precincts and dedicated them to Apollo. He begged the Delians to use the profit from this land in making sacrifices and offering gifts in his name. Then he returned to Athens, well content with himself.

The Athenians were planning an invasion of Sicily, and Nicias was one of their chosen leaders. He hoped Apollo would fight for him. Instead, Apollo fought for the Sicilians. The invasion became a rout. Nicias was captured and savagely put to death, his body being tossed over the walls as a warning to others. His army was trapped, and in the quarries of Syracuse the Athenian empire came to an end.

About this time the bronze palm tree which had been his gift to

Apollo fell over in a storm, crashed against the colossal statue of the god and hurled it to the ground. There, lying where it fell, near the sacred lake, the broken pieces remained for two thousand years.

In the reign of Charles I, Sir Kenelm Digby, a gentle and persuasive adventurer, set out on a cruise among the Aegean islands with the intention of spying out the plans of the Ottoman Empire and, to please the King, he landed on the islands and removed as many marble columns and heads of statues as he could put away in the hold of his ship. He visited Delos and paid particular attention to the Temple of Apollo. The statue was lying there broken in two pieces about the waist, and he said that though many had tried to carry it away they had all failed.

A few years later, in 1672, Segur de Vries, a Dutch painter, made a sketch of the ruins, which were still dominated by the enormous bulk of the fallen god. It is a strangely surrealist sketch, showing the colossal head still in place on the shoulders, rearing up from a forest of marble limbs and columns. Most of the statue was still there; the lime kilns had not yet begun to eat it up.

At some time during the next three years a concerted attempt seems to have been made to break up the statue. All except the trunk and part of the thighs vanished, for when Sir George Wheler and his friend the Frenchman Dr. Jacob Spon of Lyons visited Delos in 1675 the statue had become a noble ruin. Seven years later Sir George Wheler wrote a book about his travels. He was very much struck by the fallen Apollo, who was "so entirely ruin'd that it is impossible to judge as to its form, and the God himself so ill-handled that he had neither hands, feet, nor head left him; yet what is remaining appeareth still more beautiful; his locks hanging around his shoulders are yet to be seen, having marked on each curl (as we judge) where Jewels had been set, with a sign about the waste of a girdle, which had in like manner been richly adorned, and on his left shoulder a light Mantle. The statue was above four or five times bigger than Nature, and no less than a Colossus; for the shoulders are six foot broad."

Sir George Wheler was an accurate observer, always making sketches on his travels and recording inscriptions. Unfortunately he left no sketch of the statue. Yet it is clear that he saw only two huge fragments, the torso and the lower part of the body, and the torso remains today very much as he saw it. There is no trace of the mantle or the girdle, and it is very unlikely that Apollo wore either; he was nearly always depicted naked. Even today "what is remaining appeareth still more beautiful."

The learned Dr. Spon also made notes on the statue and wrote a book of his travels. He came to the same conclusions as his friend, but he added one curious piece of information. He had measured one of the thighs and found that it was nine French feet (nearly ten English feet) in circumference.

Thereafter few visitors mention the statue in any detail. We learn that about the year 1700 the lower fragment was broken up, and small pieces of it may survive anonymously in private collections in England and France, for it was a time when every young adventurer went off to the Aegean islands and accumulated relics from the ruined temples. Today there are portions of a thigh and one hand at Delos, and there is a foot in the British Museum.

The greater portion remains in Delos. There, lying where it fell, is the great torso of the god, headless, armless, broken at the waist, but still filled with tremendous power. It lies there in the open, unsheltered from the rains which will eventually reduce it to powder. It lies alone, with no great statues nearby, dominating everything in sight, splendid in its loneliness and its power.

That hulk of flashing white marble can still send the mind reeling. By the magnificent magic of time the young god, thirty feet high, has been reduced to a strange geometric proportion which conveys more power than he ever conveyed when he stood and gazed out to sea. The golden bow and the Graces were encumbrances, detracting from his beauty. All that was sensual in his gestures, the parted lips, the uplifted hands, the modeled fingers and carefully elaborated curves of belly and buttocks, have been washed away: there is only the shape of power glistening in the wheeling sunlight.

Nowhere in Delphi or in Olympia is there anything that stirs the imagination more. The torso of Olympian Zeus, if it had survived, might equal in majesty and power this shining stone; it could scarcely improve on it. The Apollo on the west pediment of the Temple of

Zeus at Olympia has majesty without power; the dew of sleep is still on him as he opens his eyes and utters his first command. He is not divine, and he is not in fact Apollo. An incomparable sweetness and nobility are conveyed by the Charioteer of Delphi, but he too is lacking in divine power; he remains the young poet eternally dreaming his life away. Only the archaic torso of the Apollo at Delos remains to remind us of the time when Greek sculptors carved their gods thirty feet high, believing that the gods deserved to be represented larger than the people who offered them sacrifices.

This archaic torso achieves the perfection of pure abstraction. It is only when you look closely that you observe the markings of the rib cage, spine and shoulderblades. Below the shoulders rounded by time falls the hair, forming a long rippling wave which is so delicately carved that unless you are standing at the proper angle it may pass unobserved. Where the huge towering neck had been there is a rough and glinting boss shaped like a wound which has healed over; this wound, and the rippling hair, give movement to the torso, which remains otherwise motionless.

More than twenty-five hundred years have passed since this colossal statue was erected on the island, but time has not weakened it. On the contrary, time has carved it into its essential proportions, removing all that is inconsequential and merely human, leaving only an austere geometric shape worthy of a divinity. Within that shape there is room for Apollo's heart to beat, there is room for shoulders to support the heavens, and there is even room for a hint of beauty in the curling hair.

THE LIONESSES

There is something about them which suggests a quivering expectancy, as though the chase were about to begin. They have the eagerness and the innocence of extreme youthfulness, and they are perhaps more dangerous for being young. They stand in a long row thirty feet apart facing the low plain, rank with weeds and wild grasses, which was once the sacred lake.

Originally there were fourteen lionesses all exactly alike, but time has reduced them to six and a solitary paw, and of these six one has been removed to guard the Arsenal at Venice. For some reason they are usually referred to as lions, but they have no manes and are obviously female. They are lean and hungry, with their jaws open.

Their youthfulness is surprising. Guardians, we feel, should be heavy and austere like the lions guarding the approaches to Karnak, or somnolent and mature like the lions in Trafalgar Square or outside the New York Public Library. They should be broad-shouldered, powerfully muscled and ripe with wisdom. But these lionesses at Delos are still wet with their mother's milk as they sit on their haunches, watching the sun.

There are no legends to account for their presence here. Lionesses are not associated with Apollo. They are associated with the Great Mother who came from Asia and who was worshiped in Crete. They appear on the royal gateway at Mycenae and on the famous Mycenean dagger which shows young lionesses at the chase; but those at Mycenae are heavy and rugged, with powerful muscles which may owe something to ancient Assyria, and those on the dagger, though lighter, cannot compare in youth with the young lionesses guarding the sacred lake.

Yet there is no need to search too far for the origin of these lionesses. In Assyria, Persia and Egypt the kings' palaces and tombs were guarded from remotest times by stone lions, and the priests of the Temple of Apollo simply followed an accepted custom, making only two significant alterations. They changed the lions to lionesses, and they made them young, full of promise, eager for the chase.

One should look carefully at those lionesses which look across the sacred lake toward Europe. Though they were carved about the same time as the stiff hieratic Apollo, who stood with one leg forward in the pose adopted from the Egyptian gods, they are charged with a youthful energy and have no stiffness at all. They are geometric forms, their long bodies like gun barrels, but they are geometry into which there has been breathed a wild and rapacious life. In them we see the expression of the European spirit with its unparalleled eagerness and thirst for adventure, its mockery of all the accepted conventions and its rage for destruction. In time those lionesses were to be unchained, and then they would go ravening through the land.

THE HIDDEN ISLAND

For nearly a hundred years French archaeologists have excavated temple after temple: so many of them, of so many periods, that the mind recoils from sheer weariness. Under the Ptolemies and later under the Romans all the lesser gods came to take shelter under the wings of Apollo, and so we find temples to Isis, to Astarte, to Cybele, to Hadad, to Atargatis, to Melqart, even to the divinities of the Ptolemaic emperors. Ovid speaks of *candida Delos* and says it was peopled everywhere with votive offerings and crowded with the gifts of kings. He was not exaggerating. The island was so sacred that the most distant gods and the most distant kings sought to share in its sanctity.

Few dared to attack the island, for the god of the golden bow was known to exact unerring vengeance on those who polluted his shrine. All nations feared the power that streamed from the barren island.

Herodotus tells the story of the Persian fleet arriving off Delos on its way to attack Greece. The panic-stricken Delians rushed down to the shore to see a thousand ships anchored in the bay, and that night, expecting a general massacre, they fled to the island of Tinos. Datis, the Persian admiral, had orders from Darius not to harm the Delians, and he quickly sent messengers to the fugitives begging them to return. "You must be out of your wits to leave such a holy place," he reminded them. "I have sense enough even without the king's orders to spare the island where Apollo and Artemis were born, and I shall do no harm to its sacred earth or its people. Therefore I beg you to return to your own homes."

As Herodotus tells the story, the Persian admiral heaped some three hundred talents' worth of incense (worth perhaps $300,000 of our money) on the altar of Apollo to placate the god for having disturbed his servants, the people of the island. The incense was solemnly burned and Datis sailed away, leaving the islanders unmolested. The next day there was an earthquake: was Apollo protesting against the coming of the Persians or against the panic of the Delians? No one knew. But they knew that some calamity would shortly be visited upon the earth.

In fact the calamity was visited on the Persians, who had dared to anchor their ships in sight of the temple of Apollo. Datis landed his men on the plain of Marathon, and his army was destroyed. Darius returned to Persia, and never again in his lifetime attempted the conquest of Greece.

Over the centuries Delos remained a place of pilgrimage, growing in sanctity. Every four years the Athenians came to perform the rites known as the Delia, their ships laden with offerings. Plays were performed, there were musical contests, sacrifices were offered and hymns were sung to Apollo and his mother Leto, "the comforter of mortal men." Games were held, and the prize was a crown of palm leaves, as at Olympia it was a crown of wild olive leaves and at Corinth it was a crown of parsley. The founder of the games was supposed to be Theseus, who had landed at Delos on his return from Crete and danced with his young Athenian companions a strange winding and twisting dance in memory of his wanderings through the Labyrinth. In memory of this prince of Athens a ship bearing a special embassy was sent to Delos each year, and during its absence no one could be put to death. Because this ship was late in returning, Socrates' life was prolonged for a few more days.

Because Apollo was the giver of swift and painless death, the sacrifices were never offered directly to him. At the Delia a hundred oxen with gilded horns were sacrificed, but none were ever offered on the bloodless altar of Apollo. On Delos no one was permitted to be born or to die: as soon as a man was seen to be evidently dying, he was hurried away to some neighboring island.

In the eyes of the Greeks, Delos was a place of exquisite purity, where there was neither mortality nor suffering, and where all things were bathed in the light of Apollo. Here everything was shining, and even the divine mysteries were hidden not in shadows but in a light that was lucid and clear, though altogether dazzling. Here there was joy beyond laughter, and a solemn happiness almost too great to be borne.

Until 146 B.C. Delos was wholly given up to the affairs of Apollo. In that year a Roman army leveled Corinth to the ground, and Delos was chosen to take its place as a free port. Apollo shared his island with the money-changers and the merchants of slaves. Strabo says the island could receive and dispatch ten thousand slaves daily, and the proverb arose: "Trader, come ashore and all are sold." Traces of warehouses and slave pens can still be seen on the northeast corner of the island. The crumbling stones are almost hidden in the barley grass, and soon they will have crumbled to powder.

Sixty years later Delos was attacked and plundered by Menophanes, an officer in the army of King Mithridates, who arrived with a fleet, put to death everyone on the island except those he sold as slaves and carried off the treasure from the temples. The Athenians derived some comfort from the knowledge that Menophanes was drowned soon afterward and the Romans hunted down King Mithridates like a wild beast.

For a few more years the slavers came to the island, but in 69 B.C. a band of pirates landed and utterly devastated it, burning what they could not carry away. Henceforward Pozzuoli, a port in southern Italy, became the center of the Mediterranean traffic in slaves.

From time to time the rites of Apollo continued to be performed. The Ptolemaic kings built palaces there, and there was a revival of the ancient worship when Augustus claimed Apollo as the patron god of his imperial line. Then gradually the island sank into obscurity. When Pausanias arrived in the second century A.D. no one was living there except the guardians sent from Athens to watch over the sanctuary of Apollo.

This was the end of Delos. Sometimes pirates gathered there, or traders took shelter in one of the three good harbors, for the island still provided the last safe anchorage before the great islands of Asia Minor. In the fourteenth century the Knights of St. John built a fortress on Mount Cynthus, but soon abandoned it. The Ottoman Turks periodically sent expeditions to the island, hurled down the statues of the gods, lopped off arms, legs and heads, and removed the marble trunks and torsos to Constantinople to reshape them into turbaned headstones. What was left over would be tossed into the lime kilns.

In time even the name of the island was forgotten. About 1624 Sir Thomas Roe, the British Ambassador to the Sublime Porte, visited the Patriarch of Constantinople and heard about a mysterious place called Delphos, "a small, despised, uninhabited island in the Arches, a place anciently esteemed sacred, the burial of all the Greeks, as yet unbroken; where, he tells me, are like to be found many rare things."

HOLINESS

There are places on the earth where holiness dwells, where benign influences rise from the earth and encompass those who walk on it. Those places are rare, and very often they are associated with crimes and sacrifices: so it is in Jerusalem, where crimes innumerable have been committed. So it is too in Delos. Apollo was born there, and his influence still spreads across the world, like the ripples when a stone is flung into a pool. He did not die. He became the young Christ, the god come to earth, the radiance of his celestial journey still about him.

One imagines he came because he was needed, because he filled some desperate need for clarity, lucidity and order. There was nothing strange in his birth, for all over Greece women gave birth standing up, holding on to a tree. Everything about him was human, and everything was divine. From his mother he acquired gentleness and patience, but in him these feminine virtues were transformed into masculine strength. He chose for his shrines the two most beautiful places in Greece, and he was the first of the gods men could strive to resemble. From him came the sense of order, the dispassionate enquiry into the nature of things, all that is adventurous and daring in man. He was the sunlight of the human mind.

While Delos owes everything to him, he in turn owes much to that island bathed in the quivering light. He has ruled over it too long to abandon it, and his presence can still be felt. It is not something born of fancy, but as concrete as rock or tree. He is present in every stone and every gleam of light, and sometimes at the turning of the ways you can catch a glimpse of him in the splendor of his nakedness, serene and smiling, strangely detached, his hands outthrust in blessing as he walks in his own marble courts. The island belongs to him still, though the excavators are at work and their narrow-gauge railroads and tipcarts wander among the ruins of great basilicas and palaces built when his worship was young.

The huge fig trees grow in the abandoned wells, and the jet planes fly overhead. The barley grows high, and the farmers come from Naxos to reap a few acres of grain, and sometimes a caïque puts in to draw water from a well belonging to a house once owned by Cleopatra. Everywhere there are movement and growth, but it is very quiet and sounds soon lose themselves. In that silence can be heard the voice of the god, calling on men to seek in themselves the lucidity of the holy light.

VI   MYCONOS

Delos is old and elemental and belongs to legend, and dazzles with its sanctity. The lean and hungry lionesses are terrifying at high noon, and there is something about the bleached bones of the ruined temples which strikes terror in the heart. Delos, one tells oneself, is the product of a completely lucid imagination, and only Apollo could have invented it. Myconos, the neighboring island, is warm and intensely human. It could have been invented by one of the lesser gods like Hercules.

Hercules indeed is associated with the island, having visited it on one of his periodic campaigns against giants. He completely defeated them and buried them so deep beneath the soil that the Greeks invented the proverb: "Everything lies below Myconos," and the lawyers came to use the phrase to describe people who treated different subjects under the same heading. There was another proverb: "He comes to a feast like a Myconiot"; it meant that the man had come uninvited. It was a poor island, all rock, with hardly a tree in sight, only remarkable because it was believed, by Pliny among others, that the islanders were born without hair. Ovid called it "humble Myconos," meaning probably that it was dull. It may have been dull then. It is not dull now.

The Chora of Myconos is the most completely beautiful town in the Aegean, and perhaps in the whole of the Mediterranean. Leave the quayside with its tumbledown hotels and tawdry souvenir shops, and you enter a forest of alleyways, all dazzling white, every house built with a consummate sense of proportion, all the planes and contours composing themselves in various degrees of whiteness. There is nothing artificial in all this whiteness. At some time during the Turkish occupation the Myconiots decided to build a town which was completely satisfying to the eyes, and they succeeded beyond all expectation.

Except for the Byzantine churches, which are permitted domes of eggshell blue or orange-pink, the entire town forms a symphony in white. Every wall, every paving stone is whitewashed. Here and there a spray of bougainvillaea hangs over a wall, or a vivid green oleander bush rises from a tub on a white balcony—the effect is shattering. I remember how in the remote village of Yenan in northern China the interminable yellow of the loess hills would catch fire if someone hung a red blanket over the mouth of a cave or if a soldier rode by with a Persian saddlecloth. So it was in Myconos, where a single flower could alter the perspective of a white street.

The unalloyed charm of Myconos lies in the discovery of so many kinds of white insensibly mingling into one another. There was greyish white, and pearly white, and blue white, and purple white. Where a bowl of roses was set in a window, there was blood-red white. There were colors whose existence I had never suspected. It was intoxicating to walk among them. It was like seeing a whole new band of the spectrum.

The town rises in a shallow amphitheater from the sea, clinging to the hills. The houses are cubes of rough stone, plastered over and then whitewashed. The cube has infinite variations. The windows are usually quite small, but they are carefully arranged, and the flatness of the cube is often broken by the outside staircases which run down with a charming candor. Since earthquakes periodically visit the Cyclades, the alleyways are often arcaded with buttresses to support the leaning houses. Occasionally a capricious balcony will dart across a street. To break any monotony the Myconiots have insisted on designing chimney pots which are pierced and patterned like lace, and they have the effect of drawing the eye upward to the intense blue sky.

There is nothing very much in the harbor except the gaily colored caïques and the flesh-colored octopus drying in the sun. There are too many cafés, too many tourists from Athens on their way to the fashionable bathing beaches. There are four excellent things on Myconos—the white town, the churches, the dovecots and the small garden behind the museum.

There are said to be 365 churches on the island, which is roughly one church for every ten people. Most of these churches are votive offerings, very small, with room for only four or five people to stand in; all of them are snow-white, and nearly all of them have pink domes. I never found two alike, and never saw one that was not designed with exquisite taste.

There are churches so small that a man can squeeze into them only with difficulty. There is a story about the tiny church dedicated to the *Panagia tou Gati*, the Virgin of the Cat. The story goes that a poor fisherman caught in a storm promised to raise a church to the Virgin if his life were preserved. By a miracle the Virgin returned him safely to Myconos, where his troubles began, for he had no money and no one would lend it to him. With his own hands he built his tiny church and placed a cross on top, but the priest refused to bless it. A cat took possession of the church and gave birth to a litter of kittens in it, and ever since it has been called the Virgin of the Cat.

The masterpiece among the churches is the Paraportiani, at the base of the southern mole. Paraportiani means "through the gates," and the gate to the city once stood here, but now all this section is falling into decay. The church is actually five churches jumbled together to form what appears to be an immense cake of melting ice cream; and simply because it is shaped in this delirious way it succeeds in catching innumerable shades of white. It stands perilously close to the sea, and all round it there is the detritus of stones from houses that have recently collapsed.

When I came up to the entrance and rattled on the rusty chain, a boy came running out of the shadows. He was about nine, with the quick dark face of an islander, very bright eyes, and a shock of glistening black hair, which disproved the thesis of Pliny that the

Myconiots were born hairless and continued hairless through their lives.

He had the key, an enormous iron key, all spikes and barbed wire, which he inserted in the gaping lock with something of the expression of a bank manager opening a vault for a favored customer. There were flourishes and smiles, and he was smiling proudly as he led me through each of the five churches, up stairways and through arched doorways. The churches were small, very dark and very dusty, but you could swing a cat in them. There were no candles, and the icons were dark and ordinary. There were no saving graces in the interior, though the exterior was a miracle.

The boy chattered away, his teeth glinting in the dark. He talked as though he would never stop. I had no idea what he was saying, until at last I was able to make him talk more slowly. Then I understood that he wanted to show me everything on Myconos, especially the churches.

"All 365 of them?" I asked, and he nodded eagerly, and burst out laughing.

He took my hand.

"You'll come fishing with me?"

"No, not today."

"Then you'll come tomorrow."

"No, I'm sailing away tomorrow."

His lips quivered. He seemed to be putting on a wonderful protestation of eternal friendship.

"Then you'll come home and meet my brother and sister?"

"No, there's no time," I said roughly. "I want to go up on the hill and see the dovecots."

He shrugged again.

"The churches are better than the dovecots," he said. "I'll take you to the Agia Eleni and to Agios Ioannis."

I let him take me to the church of Agia Eleni, which was once the cathedral of the island and has more than the usual number of gilded icons but is otherwise unremarkable. The boy was clinging to my hand. All the time he was chattering excitedly, and three-quarters of the time I could not make out what he was saying.

After the visit to the only church in Greece dedicated to St. Helena, I decided to get rid of the boy. He was too beautiful, too clinging, too insistent. I was in no mood for adventures. I gave him a tip and told him I was going up the hills alone. I remember how he stared at the tip and his lips crinkled and he fought back his tears. I still thought he was acting.

I went up along the winding roads which lead to the edge of the town. Beyond the town lie the bleak fields, a few black goats wandering distractedly. I had seen the dovecots from the shore, very white on the skyline, with their faint lacelike patterns. The road was steep, formed of immense blocks of rock almost as large as the cyclopean rocks at Delos and Mycenae. I suspect this road was very ancient, and once led from the harbor to an acropolis on the summit of the hill. Banana trees grew beside the road, and here and there lay the stubble of the summer wheat. No sounds came from the town, but an invisible shepherd was playing on his pipe.

Myconos is lovely when you walk in the white shadows of its streets, and it is just as lovely from above. The flat roofs display their varying depths of whiteness, and the curving arm of the blue bay is exactly the right shape to set off the beauty of the town. The dovecots were the loveliest of all. There were four of them scattered along the ridge. All of them were cleanly decorated, and all were crowded with doves; their cooing on that lonely ridge with the sea and the town far away was very sweet, filling the great spaces of the empty sky. The cooing went on until I threw a stone, and then there was a flutter of white and purple wings.

From the ridge Delos shone white in the sunset. Cocks were crowing, and some black goats foraged in the eternal stubble. But the strangest thing of all was an enormous white stork delicately picking its way across a tumbled wall, its white wings touched with black and therefore appropriate to an island where everything was either blinding white or in the shadows.

There was another dovecot half a mile along the ridge. It was the most beautiful of all, looking a little like a Moorish castle, pricked out with shapes like lace. It was whitewashed like all the others, but in this light it glowed with the effect of marble. Crowning it were two horns. Against the dark sky the horns stood out brilliantly. In all Myconos the most beautiful building was a dovecot set against a starry sky.

THE GARDENS

Myconos is a promise of Paradise. There comes a time when those spotless white buildings have the power to haunt the soul. Walking along those streets at noon, in the silence, you have the feeling that the world has suddenly come to an end, caught under a spell. Sometimes an old woman can be seen with bucket and brush, whitewashing the marble street, or a rubber-tired pushcart comes silently by, with water from the sweet wells in the hills. Over the whiteness and the silence the pink domes of the churches rise like a benediction.

Walking through this hushed and snowy world, it is easy to believe that ancestral memory has been at work: that the white houses reproduce on a smaller and altogether simpler scale the long-lost palaces and temples on the neighboring island of Delos, which also glittered with a blinding whiteness.

Memories and traditions in Greece survive over vast periods of time. We know, for example, that the rites of the Byzantine Church still follow many of the practices of the ancient Greek worship. There is the same separation between the congregation and the sanctuary, the same adoration of relics, the same love of processions, the same blaze of lights. Apollo has left the world, but he has not wholly vanished, for he became the young Christ.

In the end Myconos became the heir of Delos. Though Delos was a sacred island and it was not permissible for the dead to be buried there, there were periods when burials did in fact take place. The Athenians ordered the bodies dug up and moved to a necropolis on the island of Rheneia. About fifty years ago excavators in Rheneia found the necropolis and transferred the bronze sculptures, the great geometric vases and the rusted swords to the small museum at Myconos.

It is a good museum, high on a rock overlooking the crowded bay filled with scarlet caïques. It is very quiet and far from the main part of the town, and the sea's light floods through the windows. Here are jewels and jewel cases, huge alabaster urns, towering brown vases, two-handled jars which have been raised from the bottom of the sea, with the seashells still clinging to them. There is even a small fragment of the archaic Apollo from Delos. There are daggers and sacrificial knives, and a small head of Aphrodite in Naxian marble which glitters as though a candle were lit inside it. But the chief glory of the museum is a small garden filled with wildflowers, tombs and the headless gods sunning themselves in the summer air.

In the green silence of the garden the tombs lay in careful rows. There was a hollow shell which had once contained the body of a priest of Delos. There were tombstones with inscriptions in Phoenician, Greek and Latin, and languages I could not recognize; and there were many in French. The tombs of Greeks, Romans, Franks, Venetians and Turks lay there in happy and orderly confusion, all chipped and worn, slumbering in the hot sun. Altars lay there, and Corinthian columns as fresh as when they were first carved, and the birds fluttered in the bird bath formed in a hollow of one of the Frankish tombs.

I spelled out the medley of the inscriptions in languages I knew, but they were not always decipherable. Some of the Greek stones were crowned with anthemia, those delicate flowers which the Greeks always regarded as the symbol of immortality, and sometimes there was a relief showing a dead youth in his young strength. There were long inscriptions commemorating the virtues of Venetian governors. There was a simple stone reading in Greek: Philomenos cherished in Christ, farewell. There was a superb carving of a youth lying prone on the earth, and over him were the words: *Ego dormio et cor meum vigilat.* I sleep and my heart keeps watch.

There were no Christian symbols on the tomb: only the youth and the words which looked so strange in Latin, for such brevity and quiet grief seem peculiarly Greek. There was no name. Was he a Greek who had taken service under the Romans? He had been a soldier, for otherwise he would not have been shown lying on the earth, but I knew no more about him. In what century did he live, and why was he buried in the obscure island of Rheneia?

I thought of another garden behind another museum, this time at Messina. There is the same quietness, and there are more tombs and sepulchral monuments than I shall ever count. Heads of emperors and kings, vast marble urns surrounded by baroque angels, stone lions with paws upraised to protect the empty tombs. There were gold-lettered stones proclaiming the dignities received by court officials, and there were statues of kings in full panoply making commanding gestures. But there were no words which spoke so convincingly as the unknown soldier. I sleep and my heart keeps watch.

The headless gods were slung like discarded dolls against the honey-colored wall. I could not guess what happened to so many heads except that they may have been removed to the world's museums. They had the comic air of actors improvising, waiting for their heads to tumble into place again.

The shadows fell across the youth who lay so close to the earth, and soon I left the haunted garden, trying to remember a long-forgotten verse of Sophocles. I found it many months later:

> *Beyond all seas and the earth's last frontiers,*
> *The starry heavens and all the springs of Night,*
> *Apollo's ancient gardens.*

"The beautiful mask" from Mycenae

Torso of archaic statue of Apollo at Delos

Athenian tetradrachm with the Apollo of Delos shown on right, c. 150 B.C.

Painted fresco on tomb from Hagia Triadha

The lionesses at Delos

Entrance to Treasury of Atreus at Mycenae

Nikê of Paeonios   Peirithoös of Alcamenes

Lapith woman from west pediment of temple of Zeus

The "Charioteer" of Delphi

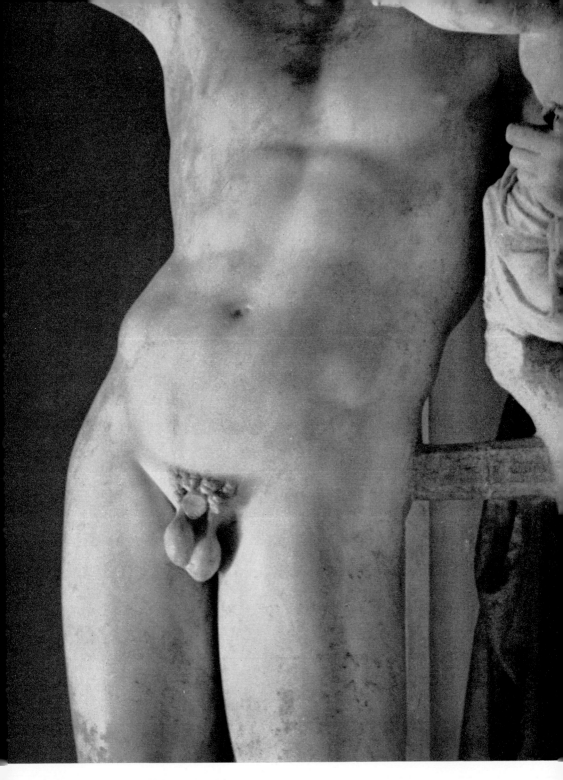

Hermes of Praxiteles

VII   C O S

It was dark when the ship reached Cos, dark and windy with a gale springing up out to sea, and the clouds were low, hiding the coast of Asia, which lay only six miles away. So we came ashore with the first dawn, which Theocritus calls "the sea-green dawn," while the sea roared against the deserted wharf. The town comes down to the sea and smells of salt spray, gasoline and dead fish. It seemed empty: it had the blank look of any small fishing town in the early morning, gaunt and shuttered and very quiet except for the fishing boats nosing each other and the sudden explosions of spray.

I remember the savage greyness of Cos at dawn, because it was the last thing I expected. I expected marble pillars and Venetian fortresses, but there was only a grey uninhabited dreariness, and a grey but without headlights standing on the wharf.

I tried to think what I could remember about this tiny island near the coast of Asia. I remembered the obvious things—Coan silk, which was worn by emperors and the most expensive prostitutes. A curious story about the death of Claudius. Wine, too—Horace especially approved of Coan wine and recommended its use, together with fried shrimps, for the very worst hangovers. Fame, indeed, hung heavily about the place. Young Greeks, and later young Romans and Alexandrians, made a point of staying at Cos, where all the refinements of civilized life could be enjoyed. Halicarnassus was only twenty miles

81

away across the sea. It was the last Greek outpost: beyond this lay Asia.

Cos, of course, suffered from its proximity to Asia and its reputation for luxury, and was periodically sacked. The island was sacred to Asclepius, the god of healing, and though it produced a school of poetry, it was most famous for having produced Hippocrates, who studied and taught medicine there in the great temple-university. Cos produced silks and wines and scented ointments, and sent them in great quantities abroad, but men remembered chiefly its prominence in medicine.

The Emperor Claudius paid tribute to the medical learning of Cos by remitting its taxes. He was nearly always falling ill, and he had a special veneration for his doctor Xenophon, who was born on the island. To please his doctor he drew up an imperial edict, naming all the most famous doctors who had practiced there from the remotest antiquity, adding a learned discussion on the influence of Coan medicine, and concluding with a brief statement on the great virtues of Xenophon, a descendant of the god of healing. Taxes were to be remitted in perpetuity: a very signal honor for the court physician, who repaid his master a few years later by giving him poison, and when the Emperor vomited up the poison Xenophon pretended to help him by inserting a feather in his throat. The feather was soaked in an even more virulent poison, and the Emperor died in agony. To this obscure doctor an ungrateful world owes the emergence of Nero.

In Cos there is no need to dwell for long on poisons. The town is ugly, having been shattered by many earthquakes, but the fields are gentle, as we discovered when the sun rose. The temple of Asclepius is only a short bus ride away. The stairways remain, and a few walls, but little more remains. The Italians removed most of the mosaics to decorate the Castello at Rhodes. There is an adorable small mosaic of fish made of very small tesserae of a startling freshness, and a few other bits and pieces of mosaic. Still, there are remains of bathhouses and dormitories, where the patients spent the night chanting while lying on the skins of the animals they had sacrificed; and sometimes into those ruined precincts there glided the sacred snakes which had the power to heal.

Those who came to the temple to be cured of their diseases seem to have been regimented like the patients in a modern hospital; and their treatment was not altogether different from the treatment they receive today. The site was chosen well, the pine forests behind the temple and the sea nearby. From the sacred spring each patient took a draught of fresh mineral water. Then the doctors examined him and prescribed a course of treatment. The patients were especially recommended to watch for visions of the night and to record them; they were recommended to have visions of the divine Asclepius, the son of Apollo. Psychological treatment of a very high order was employed, at least in the time of Hippocrates.

Who was Asclepius? His origins are lost, but he seems to have been a form of Apollo. He was Apollo grown old in the service of humanity, his features almost indistinguishable from those of Zeus. Homer calls him "the blameless physician," and all the portraits of the god suggest an old man without guile, with a passion for gentleness, tolerant of all men's abuses of their flesh.

Somewhere near here, perhaps beside the altar which once stood at the top of the threefold flight of steps, the oath known as the Oath of Hippocrates was first pronounced:

> I swear by Apollo the Healer, by Asclepius, by Health and all the powers of healing, and I call to witness all the gods and goddesses that I may keep this Oath and Promise to the best of my ability and judgment.
>
> To my master in the healing art I shall pay the same respect as to my parents, and I shall share my life with him and pay all my debts to him. I shall regard his sons as my brothers, and I shall teach them the healing art if they desire to learn it, without fee or contract. I shall hand on precepts, lectures, and all other learning to my sons, to my master's sons and to those pupils who are duly apprenticed and sworn, and to no others.
>
> I will use my power to help the sick to the best of my ability and judgment. I will abstain from harming or wronging any man.
>
> I will not give a fatal draught to anyone, even if it is demanded of me; nor will I suggest the giving of the draught. I will give no woman the means of procuring an abortion.
>
> With purity and holiness I will pass my life.

I will not cut, even for the stone, but I will leave all cutting to the practitioners of the craft.

Into whatever houses I shall enter I will go into them for the benefit of the sick and will abstain from every voluntary act of mischief and corruption; and further from the seduction of females or males, bond or free. . . .

Whatever I see or hear, either in my profession or in private, I shall never divulge. All secrets shall be safe with me.

While I continue to keep this oath unviolated, may it be granted to me to enjoy life and the practice of the art, respected by all men at all times, but should I trespass and violate this oath, may the reverse be my lot.

That extraordinary oath, first announced toward the end of the fifth century B.C., ranks with the funeral speech of Pericles among the great documents of Greek civilization. There hovers over it a sense of Apollonian calm, of a divine propriety and gentleness. By the time of Hippocrates the doctor was being regarded as a priest, possessing the privileges of a priest but also heavy responsibilities toward the gods. Doctors in those days were not specialists. Their concern was with the whole man, and they were physicians of health as well as disease.

Like Socrates, Hippocrates gives the impression of a man dedicated to the study of man as a creature of the earth and starry skies. He did not ask for supernatural explanations of men's illnesses, but he regarded men as supernatural, only a little removed from the gods, and therefore all the more worthy of being cured of their afflictions. His great collection of medical treatises—eight works are ascribed to him—shows him at work as he watches the behavior of men with a kind of quiet relish, and with amazing patience. There is nothing about men that fails to interest him. How they breathe; how they walk; how they stand; how they speak and smile; what they think, and the kind of dreams they have. It is not enough to examine the skin, the temperature, the stools, urine, sputum and vomit, all the evident signs of disease. The entire man must be seen and understood, and then after prolonged examination and after interpreting a hundred different signs it may be possible to come to some experimental conclusions concerning his health. "The examination of the body," wrote Hippocrates, "is a serious business, requiring good sight, good hearing, and sense of smell and touch and taste, and power of reasoning." By this he meant that the body was a rational organ, obeying rational laws, as the stars in their courses obey rational laws. Man was a miracle, but he was also rational.

The great achievement of Hippocrates lay in his power to sweep away the legends and present man as an infinitely complex system, each part of the system being subservient to law. He was not afraid of anatomy, and presented a perfect skeleton made entirely of gold to the Temple of Apollo at Delphi. When Plato came to compare the great men of his time it occurred to him to place Hippocrates with the great sculptors, Polyclitus and Phidias, for did not Hippocrates also shape the features of men?

The ghost of Hippocrates still hovers over the great temple at Cos. Even now, when so much of the temple has fallen in ruins, there is the sense of harmony and order, of calm achievement and quiet spaciousness. The threefold flight of steps leading to the altar with the sacred forest behind; the still-standing bathhouses and dormitories; the columns, which were all simple, unfluted and undecorated; the landscape rolling away into the blue distance—all these suggest a way of thought which was cleanly perceptive and accurate. Delphi had its marble temples set against dramatic cliffs. Here there were only the low hills and the encircling forests, and a great quietness.

It is a pity the sacred forest has gone, for one would have a better idea of the temple against a green background. There are only a few stunted pines now. Once the pines were famous for their girth, and in fact Antony gave orders that they should be cut down to build the heavy ships with which he fought the lighter triremes of Octavian, when the western and eastern halves of the Roman empire broke apart. The task of cutting down the noble trees was given to the Senator Turullius, commander of Antony's shipyards, and when Octavian marched into Egypt to destroy the empire ruled jointly by Antony and Cleopatra, Turullius was among the first to be sentenced to death. It is possible he was punished for having destroyed the sacred forest.

In Cos they show you the ancient and gnarled plane tree under which Hippocrates is supposed to have taught his pupils. It is a pleasant legend, and so far from being the truth that there are at least eight separate reasons why it is impossible. The plane tree imitates a banyan; it is swollen with a kind of dropsy, twisted and arthritic, and is shored up by a multitude of steel bars and marble columns. It is old and ready to die, and there is nothing to be said in its favor except that it must have been standing there for perhaps five hundred years. Opposite the tree stands an abandoned mosque which seems to be crumbling in sympathy.

Between the wars Cos belonged to the Italians, who set about excavating as late as 1925. They uncovered mosaic pavements and the few undistinguished statues which crowd a small museum. They regarded Cos as "the poor man's Rhodes," a makeshift place where they had no intention of putting down roots. They left their mark on Rhodes, but there is no trace of their influence at Cos. It is as though they had never been.

There are some minor mysteries about Cos. Why, one wonders, were they so old-maidish that when Praxiteles offered them a copy of his celebrated Aphrodite, modeled on the voluptuous body of his mistress Phryne, did they send it back and say they would accept it only when it was properly clothed. Apollo was less demanding. He graciously accepted the statue for his temple precincts in Delphi, and there it remained over the centuries as an example of Greek womanhood for all to observe.

Perhaps, after all, there is a very simple reason. The Coans preferred to contemplate the love of boys, and the most convincing of homosexual poems written in Greek has a Coan setting.

Theocritus wrote the *Thalysia,* or "The Winnowing," about 283 B.C. He knew the island well, having spent most of his youth there. In the poem he describes how he was once walking with two friends from the town of Cos to a harvest festival at a farm six or seven miles away. On the way they fell in with a young goatherd:

His name was Lycidas. Over his shoulder
He wore the tawny skin of a thick-haired goat,
All shaggy, reeking of fresh curd; around his breast
An ancient well-worn tunic which was belted
With a broad belt; in his right hand
He waved a crooked club from a wild olive tree.
So, smiling gently, his eyes alight with laughter,
He said: "Well, poet, where goest thou in the hot noonday?
The lizards sleep, and even the crested larks
Are silent in their nests, and yet thou art
Swaggering abroad. Goest thou feasting?"

The poet explains that he is not going to any ordinary feast. He is going, he says, to the harvest festival of Demeter of the Fair Robes: there will be songs, and much wine, and Theocritus hopes he will win the prize for poetry. So they walk together along the road, and to while away the time the handsome goatherd sings a song in honor of a young friend, and Theocritus, in no mood to be beaten by a simple goatherd, sings a song in honor of *his* friend. Lycidas is so pleased with the song that he gives Theocritus his club as a pledge of friendship.

That is all, or nearly all, for in the poem Theocritus never reaches the harvest festival. For a little while longer the friends wander along the road and at last they turn into a field and lie down in the shade. No one has ever written so well about the happy weariness of young men taking shelter from the sun:

There at last we lay
On beds of scented rushes and fresh vine-leaves,
While elms and poplars murmured overhead.
From the Cave of the Nymphs came the whisper of a spring,
And from the shady boughs came the chatter of dusky cicadas.
The voice of the turtle echoed from the thick thorn-brakes,
Doves were moaning, larks and finches were singing,
While over the running water hovered the bees.
Pears fell at our feet, apples rolled at our sides,
All things were fragrant with harvest and ripeness ...

One thinks of the Hermes of Praxiteles. It is all a little too luxuriant, a little too ripe. Milton admired the poem and borrowed the name of Lycidas from it. The historian Macaulay preferred it above all other pastoral idylls, and seems not to have understood half its implications.

In the years since Theocritus, little has changed. The boys wander arm in arm through the streets of the Chora. When the warm winds come in from the sea Cos returns to its ancient luxuriance.

VIII   D E L P H I

The story is told that when Apollo left the holy island of Delos to conquer Greece, a dolphin guided his ship to the little town of Crisa beneath the Shining Cliffs. The young god leaped from the ship disguised as a star at high noon; flames soared from him and the flash of splendor lit the sky; and then the star vanished, and there was only a youngster armed with a bow and arrows. He marched up the steep road to the lair of the dragon who guarded the cliffs, and when the dragon was slain he announced in a clear ringing voice to all the gods that he claimed possession of all the territory he could see from where he was standing. He was among other things the god of good taste, and he had chosen the loveliest view in Greece.

It is a haunting view, and no one has quite succeeded in explaining why it is so intensely satisfying. There is the faint blue sea in the distance and a valley of grey-blue olive trees below and blue mountains curving away to left and right, and the Shining Cliffs rise protectively behind; and there is a kind of quietness and composure in the scene, the sense of a complete world—streams, mountains, plains, wide spaces of sky and sea—effortlessly displayed. It is a bitter place in winter when the mists pour off Parnassus, but for nine months of the year it is a gentle place. Standing near the temple of Apollo you have the impression that the valleys and the mountains and the sea are slowly revolving around the fulcrum of the Shining Cliffs, which reach a thousand feet above your head, implacably stern and remote. The eagles fly above the cliffs, and their shadows leap like wild things across the plain.

For his home in Greece, Apollo chose a saddle in the hills, which could be reached only by a long and laborious climb from the sea or across the arid foothills of Parnassus. His pilgrims would come to him exhausted by a healthy fatigue and therefore all the more inclined to gratitude when they came in sight of the white and gold glory of his temple. He ordered them to come in high summer, when the scorching sunlight flashes off the rocks. Mostly they came very slowly, following the winding road from the port of Itea. On a single day fifty thousand pilgrims streamed through the port, where today there is hardly a single visitor.

Except for a few pitiful columns nothing remains of the temple of Apollo. The golden statues have gone, and the *adyton* where the Pythia uttered prophecies is a rubble of foundation stones. The French excavators who cleared the site by removing an entire village from the sacred precincts had hoped to find more. They found innumerable inscriptions, ruined treasuries, the ground plan of an entire temple-city, but not one single intact statue. Except for the Charioteer they found nothing comparable to the great German discoveries at Olympia. Characteristically the French always sought to dig in the territory of Apollo; both Delos and Delphi were excavated by them. The Germans chose Mycenae and Olympia, which is sacred to Zeus, a more ponderous god than the young lighthearted master of the waves. The Italians with the encouragement of Mussolini chose Phaestos. Knossos was chosen by the English, and the Americans worked with them in Athens. Each nation found something of itself in ancient Greece.

The foundations of the temple are still impressive. The white stone gleams like fire. It commands the ridge like a command post. It was not the first temple to be erected there. The first was a very small shrine, made of beeswax and feathers; the second of ferns twisted together; the third of laurel boughs; the fourth of bronze with golden songbirds perched on the roof; the fifth of stone, which was burned in 489 B.C.; the sixth was destroyed in an earthquake in 373 B.C.; the seventh was plundered and then torn down by the Christian Emperor Arcadius about A.D. 398. It was built of Sikyon limestone, which has a pleasant clear whiteness and a quiet steady glow.

Arcadius gave it the death blow, but it was already falling into ruins in the second century A.D. Pausanias tells of coming to the sanctuary and finding it deserted. Some temples were in ruins; others had lost their statues. Once the cypress groves surrounding the temple were crowded with bronze portraits of gods and heroes. Nero removed seven hundred of them and sent them to Rome. It was the beginning of the end. Delphi survived for a few more centuries, but the heart seems to have gone out of it. Apollo had been dying ever since the Romans became the masters of Greece.

Apollo died, but he was a long time dying. When the Gauls attacked Delphi he filled the air with his lightning and threw them into wild panic. They heard horses riding against them when there were no horses; every man thought he saw an enemy beside him, and so they threw themselves at one another's throats. Sleet and snow fell, and huge crags toppled over the edge of Parnassus and crushed them. But though Apollo could destroy the Gauls, he was helpless before the leaden march of the Roman legionaries.

Augustus Caesar believed himself to be the servant of the god and built a great temple for him on the Palatine; and when the poet Horace thought to please the Emperor he called him "Apollo's slave." Only one Roman emperor truly believed in the young god. This was Julian the Apostate, who visited the shrine in A.D. 362 on the eve of his disastrous campaign in Persia. He asked what he could do to preserve the glory of the god. Then for the last time, in words of almost intolerable sweetness, the voice of the oracle was heard:

> *Tell the King the fair-wrought house has fallen.*
> *No shelter has Apollo, nor sacred laurel leaves;*
> *The fountains now are silent; the voice is stilled.*

THE ORACLE

When I was younger and knew with great certainty many things about ancient Greece which now seem to me very dubious, I thought I knew all about the oracle at Delphi. Somewhere near the great temple of Apollo there was a cave, and poisonous gases mounted through a fissure in the rock, enveloping the Pythia who sat on a bronze tripod. The poisonous gases were supposed to come from the eternal decomposition of the Pytho, the dragon slain by Apollo. The priestess inhaled the gases and fell into convulsions, and thus inspired, uttered the strange poems which were later carried to the four corners of the earth as prophecies and warnings. Sometimes I remembered that she was supposed to chew sacred laurel leaves, but whether this was before or after she sat on the tripod and inhaled the gases I never knew, nor greatly cared.

There is only one trouble about the conventional account of the Delphic oracle: there is not the slightest evidence that anything remotely resembling it ever took place. There was no cave, and there were no gases. One can chew a very large number of laurel leaves without getting anything worse than a bad headache. The priestess sat in the temple, and it is very unlikely that she was drugged.

What did in fact happen, as we learn from the pages of Plutarch, was at once more exciting and far less spectacular. In his day the Pythia was the daughter of a poor farmer, a perfectly respectable young woman of honest upbringing, but with little education. She was trained in the priesthood and observed all the rites and vigils appropriate to the worship of Apollo. On the day of the oracle she bathed in the Castalian spring, put on the special robes of prophecy, and was led to the Temple of Apollo, passing through the main halls of worship until she reached the *adyton*, the most sacred part of all, the living place of the god where only the priests were allowed to enter.

Here she took her place on a tripod or a throne, and she may have taken a branch of holy laurel in her hands or perhaps she fumigated herself with burnt laurel leaves, for at Delphi the laurel was sacred to Apollo. Music was played, and incense was burned. In the dark chamber all eyes were fixed on the young priestess who had assumed the robes and insignia of the god. Very quickly she fell into a trance, succumbing to the overwhelming influence of suggestion, the knowledge that the god was present in her. At her feet was the sacred *omphalos*, the stone phallus covered with mysterious ribbons, and before her eyes stood a golden image of the god.

Only the priests were present; their task was to ensure that she was "possessed" by the god. It was probably not very difficult, for they placed in her hands one of the sacred ribbons which bound her to the *omphalos*, believed to be the center of the universe and the source of all creative power, and they gave her every encouragement to speak as a god might speak. Blinded by the gleam of the golden statue, charged with the energy of the *omphalos*, numbed by the music, the incense and the repetitive prayers of the priests, she uttered wild and frenzied words which were carefully taken down, and later a priest put them into verse.

It did not always, of course, happen quite like that. Plutarch tells the story of a priestess who went into a trance reluctantly and in a state of depression, because the omens were unfavorable. She was distressed, spoke in a hoarse voice, and was filled with "a dumb and evil spirit"; in the end she rushed screaming to the door and fell to the ground, whereupon the priests fled in terror. When they recovered from their panic, they returned and carried her away. She seemed to have completely recovered, but a few days later she died suddenly.

Plutarch probably learned the story from his friend, the priest Nicander, who was actually present at the scene. The story rings true. Such failures of nerve very often happen during states of trance, and we have the authority of the New Testament for believing that people can be possessed by evil spirits. Plutarch's story is important because it tells us that the trance was still regarded as a genuine phenomenon in his day, and we need not suppose it was less genuine when Chaerophon, the boyhood friend of Socrates, asked the Pythia: "Is there anyone wiser than Socrates?" and received the answer: "There is no one."

We shall never know exactly what transpired in the *adyton* or what went through the mind of the priestess when she was "possessed" by the god, or what sources of energy were tapped by those simple farm girls who permitted themselves to become the vehicles of the god. Perhaps they tapped the collective unconscious ideas of the priests, but it is more likely that they performed an act of perfect surrender to Apollo and for a brief space believed themselves to be incarnations of the god. The example of Joan of Arc should warn us against believing that farm girls are incapable of talking with the tongues of angels.

We know that cheating sometimes took place, for Herodotus tells the story of how Cleomenes suborned the priestess Perialla and received from her the reply he wanted, but he gained no advantage from the deed, which soon became known. The priestess was punished by being deprived of her office; no other punishment is recorded. But these occasions were rare, and there seems to have been very little attempt by the priests to falsify the utterances made by the priestess in her trance. For at least nine hundred years the oracle at Delphi was held in great reverence by the Greeks, who believed that Apollo spoke through the lips of the Pythia.

The prestige of the oracle survived its astonishing behavior during the Persian War, when it openly counseled surrender to the enemy. The priestess Aristonikê promised the Athenians "absolute ruin when fire and the headlong god of war coming in a Syrian chariot shall entirely overwhelm you." The perplexed Athenians sent more envoys to the priestess, this time with olive boughs, hoping for a less relentless fate. This time they were told: "Divine Salamis will bring death to women's sons when the corn is scattered or the harvest gathered in." But what was meant by "divine Salamis"? who were "the women's sons"? why at the time of the scattering of corn? what was the harvest?

The professional interpreters explained the prophecy as a Greek defeat at Salamis. Themistocles believed it pointed to victory, for otherwise Salamis would not have been called "divine." So it turned out, and the Persians were scattered, and the harvest fell to the Greeks.

Not all the Delphic oracles were so devious. Sometimes there was an almost childlike directness in the utterances of the Pythia. King Croesus asked the oracle whether he would succeed in his conquests, and was told: "Cross the river Halys, and you will destroy a great empire." He crossed the river, and destroyed his own empire. Some colonizers were told: "Seek for the blind men," and when they sailed toward the Black Sea they observed that colonizers before them had built a city at Chalcedon, overlooking the Golden Horn, which had a better harbor and was altogether more desirable. They decided that "the blind men" were the people of Chalcedon. When Hadrian asked the Pythia for the birthplace of Homer, he was told: "In Ithaca. Homer was an immortal Siren, Telemachus his father and his mother Nestor's daughter." It was a charming theory, and at least as plausible as those invented later by professors.

Nearly all the surviving oracles contain a germ of happy childlike improvisation, like a child speaking its dreams aloud. Their authenticity derived perhaps from the collective unconscious married to a virginal innocence; like the Chinese *Book of Changes* they formed riddles which were capable of many solutions, including sometimes the only proper solution.

Apollo ruled the Greek world for centuries, speaking through the lips of a young girl in a white temple high up in the hills above the Crisian plain. He was—the words were spoken by Aeschylus—the vicar on earth of the Heavenly Father, messenger and divine evangel of Zeus. He was sometimes wrong, but against his commands, his prophecies, his least utterances there was no appeal, for everything that was touched with the morning light belonged to him. They kept faith with him if for no other reason than that he was the most *apparent* of the gods, visible in the Shining Cliffs at Delphi and in every stone and pebble of the white island of Delos.

THE CHARIOTEER

I first saw the Charioteer of Delphi shortly after the Second World War in the National Museum at Athens: he had been removed only a few weeks before from a hiding place in the hills. He stood in a large room, in a corner, with the air whirling around him, dominating everything in sight, larger than life, unmistakably living, wearing his green patina like another robe over his rippling gown. There was about him a sense of incomparable grandeur and also of vigor, as though this dreaming youth would in a moment transform his dreams into action: that fierce aristocratic vigor which the photographs fail to capture. He was at his ease, yet tense. The faintest of smiles hovered on his lips. He was very young, and he had the energy of youth. Seeing him there, so young and so vivid, one had the curious impression that he alone seemed to know where he was going.

Today the Charioteer has been removed to his ancestral home in Delphi. He is no longer shown in a large room, but stands nearly at the end of a long narrow corridor, dramatically highlighted. The air no longer whirls around him, and he no longer exists in space, in the free running space which was his before. He is the most precious object in the Delphi museum, and so the directors have made sure that we shall not overlook him and they have told us exactly how we should direct our gaze at him. It is a pity. He needs air. He needs space. In Delphi he seems to be suffocating. Here everything that is exquisite and aristocratic about him is underscored, and everything that is human about him vanishes in the jeweled setting.

The lower part of the statue, the long fluted skirt, was found by French archaeologists on April 28, 1896, after the rubble at the foot of the theater had been washed away in the spring rains. The skirt and the beautifully formed feet were found undamaged. During the following days, working with feverish excitement, they found a piece of a stone base recording its dedication by Polyzalos, the brother of the tyrant Hiero of Syracuse. They also found fragments of a chariot pole, two hind legs of horses, a horse's tail, a hoof, fragments of reins and the arm of a child. At last on May 1st they found the upper part and the right arm some thirty feet away, higher up and closer to the theater. They were not damaged, but heavily corroded by moisture from a sewer. During the next days they searched for the missing arm, which was never found. What surprised them more than anything else was the extraordinary state of its preservation. Nothing except the arm was lost. Greek artists were known to have concentrated on the eyes, but no one had ever seen the fully modeled eyes of a monumental Greek statue as it left the hands of the sculptor.

The whites of his wide-open eyes were of enamel, and the pupils were of onyx. The eyelashes, spikes of thin bronze, were inserted above and below the eyes. The teeth, barely visible between the lips, were represented by a strip of silver. Everything about the face suggests a portrait. There is no modeling of the body, which is hidden beneath stiff hieratic folds, but the hands and feet are scrupulously modeled, showing every vein, every curl and twist of muscle. They are slender aristocratic hands with something childlike about them, but the feet with the long toes suggest a man who has run many races.

He stands there in his dreaming youth, so young that there is no down on his cheeks, a boy of perhaps fourteen who has overreached his strength, gazing impassively before him, with the faintest suggestion of disdain in those lips which are too full, that beauty which is a little too self-regarding. He is evidently a prince, and we know that the youthful Syracusan princes did take part in chariot races. But is he a charioteer?

The only evidence we have comes from the ribbonlike reins, found some distance away, which fit snugly in his hands. We are told by the French archaeologists that the charioteer formed part of a great monumental sculpture showing the victory of a Syracusan tyrant, either Hiero or Gelo, in the Pythian games, the tyrant and the horses and perhaps the chariot itself being represented in marble. We are told that there were four horses, and these together with the chariot were set on a high stone plinth. We are also told that the unknown sculptor is especially to be commended because he carved the feet so flawlessly, although no human eye would ever see them.

I think this is nonsense. No one who has ever looked carefully at those lean and muscular feet, every toe filled with its own living energy, can imagine that it was ever placed high up. The feet, like the hands, were meant to be seen at eye level. They were made lovingly and accurately by a sculptor who wanted them to be seen, because they formed part of the intricate design of the whole, of the strange rippling music which is partly expressed in the long deep folds of the gown and the slender pizzicato folds of the sleeves. There is deliberate hieratic stiffness, but there is also movement—a gentle swirling movement: the gown has fallen in heavy folds, but in a moment it will move in the wind. Everywhere there are felicities. Across the shoulders the stuff of the long chiton is gathered in a curious arrangement of threads, so as not to impede the movement of the arms, and very intricate wavelets are introduced. The bunching of the top of the chiton, the hair curling delicately from under the headband, the damp curls on the perfectly rounded head, all these suggest that the sculptor designed the statue for a close view. Visitors to Delphi could walk past and round him. He was a Syracusan prince, but he was also an image of Apollo, standing in the familiar Apollonian position with the arms thrust forward and bent at the elbows. He may have been holding a laurel wreath.

Remove the reins—those ribbons of twisted bronze which have been slipped into the one remaining hand—and he is no longer a charioteer. He is a youth performing an act of worship or a divinity making an offering.

It happens that we know exactly where the statue was found—in the filling of a supporting wall which had been built above the Temple of Apollo to prevent rock and scree from falling into the temple precincts. The statue probably fell in the great earthquake of 372 B.C. It must have rolled down until it fell against the supporting wall and was then covered with rubble. I suspect that it stood at the top of the stone stairway leading from the Temple of Apollo to the theater, and the visitor would see it at first as a dark silhouette against the sky and then, when he had climbed the stairs, he would see it at close quarters.

No one knows who carved the statue. It has been ascribed to Pythagoras of Rhegium, who, according to Pliny, was the first to pay careful attention to sinews, veins and hair, and the first to aim for rhythm and symmetry. Everything we know about Pythagoras of Rhegium suggests an originator, a man who stands at the beginning of the classical age in sculpture. There are archaic elements in the statue, but there is also the deliberate use of the archaic for a more modern purpose: there are complexities in those draped folds which go beyond anything known up to that time. The statue has the freshness which comes only at the beginning of a new movement.

There was fire and energy in him once, when he stood in the open under the Shining Cliffs. Now he is coffined in a museum and stands in his small rotunda at the end of a long corridor, as though he were an Aphrodite who must be given an exquisite setting.

There is something to be said for throwing down the walls of the museum and letting him stand in the air again.

THE EAGLES

When Flaubert came to Delphi, he was struck by the awful silence of the place, the misery and the splendor. In his day the temple of Apollo and all the other temples were hidden by the village of Kastri, a huddle of some thirty houses built on the foundations of huge monoliths, and there were only a few scattered columns in the fields. But the place moved him deeply. *"Avoir choisi Delphes, pour y mettre la Pythie, est un coup de génie,"* he wrote. *"C'est un paysage à terreurs religieuses."*

It is still a place of religious terror, especially in the evening when the moon gathers strength and the mist floods the valley, so that the sacred precincts seem to be floating over vast and mysterious chasms. It is best in moonlight; best of all when the moon is just breaking. Then there is enough light to see, and not enough to be blinded by that forest of marble, those endless broken walls and strange shapes of rock. In the moonlight all of Delphi acquires form and grace. There are times, especially at high noon, when it looks like an abandoned quarry cut on the edge of the cliffs.

I remember climbing in the moonlight beyond the temple along the steep curving path which leads to the theater. The wolves were howling on Parnassus, and the dogs barked in the shuttered village below; and the air was full of the scent of wild thyme, very clean, and I could hear water flowing. Sometimes a black lizard, basking in the moonlight, jumped away at the sound of my footfalls, but more often the lizards remained motionless. Eagles wheeled above the Shining Cliffs. There was something raw and desolate about the evening: the cold white mists, the jagged stones.

It was a very small theater, and according to the guidebooks a comparatively modern one, having been built originally in the fourth century B.C. and then rebuilt in the second century by King Eumenes II, who is one of my favorite kings. He built the great altar of Zeus at Pergamum with its vast reliefs of the gods in attitudes of happy torment, and he built a vast library which Antony captured and presented to Cleopatra. All, or nearly all, the books in the library were written on skins, and we owe the word "parchment" (*charta pergamena*) to the invention of his librarians. Eumenes II was always making gifts, and the most pleasant of all was a covered portico which he set up near the theater at Athens to prevent theater-goers from having to stand in the pouring rain while waiting for tickets.

Eumenes II delighted me, and so did the theater, but the view from the theater over the ruins and valleys was still more delightful. The moonlight gave solidity to the low, broken walls. It was possible to make out the complete shape of the temple of Apollo, very white, with its three separate chambers, and the zigzag path which climbed up the mountainside and came to an end only when it reached the portals of the temple. Everywhere there were stones and columns, altars and treasuries and huge boulders, and they followed an intelligible pattern. There was the stone plinth on which once stood the gold chariot of the Sun given by the people of Rhodes, and further away beyond the temple of stones was a rough circle forming the ancient Threshing Floor, which was not a threshing floor but a meeting place of the elders of Apollo's church. It was as though a great wind had come and thrown the walls flat, sending bricks and stones flying, so that some of them were at incredible distances down the hill, while others remained exactly where they had fallen. In the moonlight they shone like crystal, and they acquired a strange life when clouds crossed the moon and threw shifting shadows over the sanctuary.

Far, far below, the moon-blanched olive trees shone in a silver mist, and the sea glimmered beyond the rock slopes and the grey precipices and the long winding path. There was the valley, and the rolled-down stones, which were scattered like the stars in the sky.

Once it was a place of order, where everything was appropriately placed, because it was unthinkable that there should be disorder in the presence of Apollo. At night it acquired shape and form and substance. Once again there were the shining palaces of the god on the edge of the cliffs.

I had not expected this. I had expected to be conscious of the great beetling crags of the Phaedriades, but they were invisible, swallowed up in the darkness. I had expected to be aware of height, of being far above the sea on some elevated and almost unreachable ledge below Parnassus, but there was no impression of height: the sanctuary forms a world of its own, the slopes vanish in the moonlight. That lonely eminence becomes a walled city in the plain of the night.

It was something else on the way down. Even though the moon came out round and full, throwing a shimmering icy whiteness on the whole valley, the descent was gruesome. It was like climbing down the bed of a dried-up river, blinding white. Pebbles slithered underfoot. From the top of the theater everything had seemed calm, peaceful, arranged in order, but there was no calm descent. It was terrifying. The huge foundation stones of the temple were so massive that it might have been Mycenae. Reliefs, statues, columns, stone outcrops formed a stone jungle. There was no way out, and the journey seemed to go on forever, and I thought I heard the wolves on Parnassus. I remember looking up suddenly and seeing a headless statue. From every rock and every stone came the blinding reflection of the moonlight.

By the time I reached the hotel I had two bloody ankles and all the dogs of Kastri were barking.

EVA SIKELIANOS

She was one of those rare women who possess the power of raising the dead. She was small and slight, with long red hair which reached halfway down her back, and a face that was at once patrician and childlike, with heavily lidded eyes and wonderfully clear brows. She talked in a very deep voice, and no one who ever saw her felt that she belonged entirely to this world. She was born Eva Palmer in New York, the daughter of a millionaire. She died in self-chosen poverty in Athens and is buried in Delphi high above the theater of Eumenes, with the brilliant stones of Apollo's temple guarding the approaches to her tomb.

"She was the only ancient Greek I ever knew," a modern Greek actress told me. "She had a strange power of entering the minds of the ancients and bringing them to life again. She knew everything about them—how they walked and talked in the marketplace, how they latched their shoes, how they arranged the folds of their gowns when they arose from table, and what songs they sang, and how they danced, and how they went to bed. I don't know how she knew these things, but she did!"

There are no books about her, and as far as I know no account, of any length, of her extraordinary life has been published. She wrote a few short articles, mostly about the Greek theater. They were written toward the end of her life, and there is no fire in them, no hint of her extraordinary powers, nothing to suggest how she singlemindedly went about re-creating the past.

She was a sickly child, and the doctors gave little hope that she would grow to maturity. She read omnivorously, studied under tutors, and recovered her health sufficiently to go to Bryn Mawr and then to the Sorbonne. In Paris she met the Duncans, Isadora and Raymond, who had both fallen under the spell of ancient Greece. Raymond Duncan's wife was a slender dark-eyed Greek girl who decided that Eva would make the perfect wife for her brother Angelos Sikelianos, a young poet of remarkable achievement and disturbing beauty.

Eva Palmer became Eva Sikelianos after a fashionable marriage at the home of her parents in Bar Harbor, Maine. She adored her husband, rushed back to Greece with him, visited his home on the island of Lefkas, fell in love with the islanders and settled in Athens. She learned Greek, and wrote and spoke the language so well that she could be taken for a Greek. Angelos celebrated the ancient Greek gods in modern verse: vast rhapsodic splashes of verse which sometimes harden into a vivid austerity. He was a good poet, but an uneven one. Eva, who looked like a small red-haired Athene, became his muse.

Shortly after the First World War, Angelos Sikelianos developed the idea that the spiritual capital of the ancient world was Delphi, and he urged a revival of the Delphic games. He invited artists of all kinds and all men of good will to assemble there every year, so that in some mysterious way the influence of Apollo would fall upon them. He dreamed of an intellectual *élite* which would somehow rule the world from Delphi. He had vast and grandiose schemes for reviving the worship of the Greek gods. He was the poet, remote and aristocratic, a little embittered, dreaming of an ancient grandeur which had vanished forever.

Eva was more practical. She shared many of her husband's beliefs, but her chief interest lay in reviving the drama. Greek tragedies in modern translation were of course being acted, but haphazardly with no attempt to recapture the original mood. She threw herself into the study of everything pertaining to ancient drama. What did the actors wear? How did they hold themselves? Were the choruses choreographed? Did the choruses sing to music, and if so, what music? What was the role of the chorus? How were the ancient dramas directed? There were a thousand questions, and she set about answering all of them.

She was not a great scholar. Her tools were intuition, patience, the faculty of being able to immerse herself wholly in her task. She believed that Byzantine music was a development of ancient Greek music, a belief which is not borne out by the surviving fragments of ancient music. She believed that it was possible to work out the choreography of ancient dances by studying the postures in the figured drawings on ancient vases. By studying the folds of the robes, she invented an entirely new theory of how they were worn, and of what material they were made, and she set about weaving these robes for actors on her own loom. She devised a complete presentation of the *Prometheus Bound* of Aeschylus, in which she was at once producer, director, choreographer, stage designer, chorus master, composer and dressmaker.

She was the guiding spirit of the First Delphic Festival, which opened in May, 1927, with great fanfare. There were games and exhibitions of folk art. There was also the long-promised performance of *Prometheus Bound*, on which she had been working for three years.

The performance stunned the Greeks. For the first time they saw a completely convincing performance of an ancient tragedy, with no compromises with modern taste. It flowed directly from Aeschylus through the shaping mind of Eva Sikelianos onto the stage. The years rolled away, and once more Prometheus was chained to the rock calling upon the heavens to avenge him; and at the moment when he cried out in the greatest agony, his voice thundered and reverberated against the Phaedriades. This was an effect she had not counted on, or believed possible. Many wept at the beauty of that voice, and they wept again when two eagles swooped down from the Phaedriades and circled the stage and the audience and soared away.

She had shown what could be done with tact, imagination and taste, but she had spent her inheritance on the production. There was no money left. She lived quietly with her husband, who was almost as improvident as she was. She spent the war years in New York, but she was always miserable when separated from Greece. At last in 1952 she flew back to Greece like someone returning to her own home. She was already dying when she came to Delphi. She took her place in the seat of honor at the theater, applauded the actors, gazed up at the wheeling eagles in the sky; and sometimes, even at the theater which she loved above all things, she would fall into a quiet sleep.

Feasts were given in her honor. The people of Delphi crowded round her. They remembered the time when she had made Delphi famous. From all over the world people had come to attend the festivals, usually at her expense. One evening, during a feast, she fell unconscious. She never recovered. They placed a pomegranate in her hand and a coin between her lips and carried her up to the graveyard high above the temple. Then she entered the radiance of Apollo, which the Greeks know as *Heliou Basileuma*, the kingdom of the Sun.

IX   AEGINA

There was a time when all over the eastern Mediterranean men spoke in fear of this island. Once it was a great power with shipyards, fleets and armies, a vast banking system, schools of athletes and sculptors and temple builders. It sent embassies to the Pharaohs of Egypt. It produced the first coins ever minted in Europe, and the heavy Aeginetan drachma stamped with a sea-tortoise remained for centuries the standard currency on the mainland. These islanders were the best sailors in Europe, and they supplied more ships in the Persian wars than any state except Athens.

There must have been Aeginetan historians, but none of their works have survived. In 459 B.C., twenty years after Salamis, the Athenians conquered the island and because they were afraid of the islanders' skill they ruthlessly banished every last one and resettled the land with Athenians. Among those who were given grants of land from the conquered territory were the families of Plato and Aristophanes.

The Athenians were in a merciless mood. They destroyed an entire culture. They took over the banks and shipyards, and reduced the island to the status of a suburb of Athens. Pericles called Aegina "the eyesore of Piraeus"—it is one of the few authentic phrases known to have been spoken by him—and in a burst of barbaric violence he ordered that the thumbs of the Aeginetans be hacked off, for fear that even in exile they would use their spears and bows again.

It is a pleasant island, thick with pines and fig trees and small farms, and there is something intensely masculine in the heavy shapes of the ochre-colored mountains. Once Lucian took a group of friends to Aegina from Athens in a small boat at four obols a head in order to see the islanders celebrate the festival of Hecate; and it took him a whole day. I made the journey in an hour in a fast Swedish motor vessel which was very low on the water, very white, beautifully proportioned, as sleek as the dolphins rolling in the Bay of Salamis.

The main town of all the Greek islands is called "Chora," meaning "the place." The main town of Aegina is far from Athens and for perhaps half an hour you coast along the lowlands called Plakakia, where the Greek poet Kazantzakis lived out his long exile in a small whitewashed house overlooking the waterfront. Beyond the lowlands lie the mountains crowned by the high peak of Oros, once the sanctuary of Zeus Panhellios, now bearing the inevitable chapel to St. Elias, who haunts so many of the summits of Greek mountains that one suspects he has a preference for the upper air.

There are few places in Greece more delightful than the harbor filled with gaily painted caïques, the blue-washed, twin-domed chapel of St. Nicholas at the end of the long breakwater. It is a tiny chapel, hardly larger than a peasant's hut, but all the light of the surrounding sea breaks upon the eggshell blue of the domes.

Of the once-great city of Aegina nothing remains: no walls, no theaters, no columns. To the north a mile away from the Chora stands a single fluted column, all that survives of a temple erected on the headland to Aphrodite. The column has been worn to a point and is in danger of falling, but in its place, above that rough headland, it admirably fulfills the function of columns to illuminate and point a landscape. The air washes around it; the sea seems to move toward it; and Aphrodite is well served.

There is nothing to see in the town except two horrible churches, which are worth visiting for the same reason that one visits a Chamber of Horrors. They have the proper number of icons, and no doubt the proper services are performed in them, but they have a bleakness and emptiness unusual among Greek churches. There is none of the dark mystery and dusky gold of the usual Byzantine churches. These churches are solid and temperate and chapel-like; and it is good to escape into the narrow dusty streets, and then into the vineyards.

Aegina is far richer than most of the Greek islands. It has good clay for making pottery; long stands of pinewood; some dairy farming; vineyards, cornfields, orchards. The figs, which are lemon-colored with juicy purple centers, are particularly succulent. When I think of Aegina I remember the juicy figs and the scent of the pinewoods and the fat donkeys delicately treading the mountain paths. Fat donkeys are always a good sign in Greece.

Aegina is famous above all for the temple of Aphaia which lies on the other side of the island. To reach the temple you take the bus, which whirls along a wild dusty road climbing past orchards of pistachio trees until it reaches a narrow valley. The valley opens out theatrically to display the huge grey fortresslike rock of Palaeochora with its ruined white churches hugging the slopes.

Palaeochora is a mountain shaped for romantic grandeur, a great gnarled shoulder against the sky. Once a whole city clambered up the slopes. Once there were fortress walls and sally ports, and in the church lay the head of St. George in a golden casket. Under the Byzantines, Palacochora was the capital of the island, being out of the reach of pirates. The pirates, of course, invaded it from time to time. When the Crusaders conquered Constantinople, it passed into the hands of the Venetians and then from one Frankish Lord to another. For a while it was owned by Otho de Cicon, that exemplary soldier who lent five thousand ducats to a Latin Emperor, receiving one of the arms of John the Baptist as surety. The Catalans took possession of the mountain, and were followed by the Venetians, who removed the precious head of St. George to San Giorgio in Venice, where it remains to this day.

The Venetians were always stern taskmasters in the eastern Mediterranean. They built fortifications intended to endure across the centuries, and when they took possession of a town they destroyed the title deeds of previous owners. The story is told of how the Aeginetans on Palaeochora were in tears when they received the visit of a Venetian general. They complained that the Venetian commander who had taken charge of the city had no conception of democratic rule. They had shown him their patents of nobility, their land deeds and their hereditary privileges. The commander quietly placed these documents in a sack, and some time later he solemnly handed the documents back to them. The mice had nibbled them, and not a single document could be read. The Aeginetans threatened to emigrate *en masse*, and the Venetian general laughed.

It might have been better if the Aeginetans had been allowed to emigrate. In 1537 the fleet of Suleyman the Magnificent came in sight of Aegina. Four days later a landing party under the command of the infamous Barbarossa attacked Palaeochora. He destroyed the town, butchered all the men and carried 6,000 women and children off to slavery. A few years later when a French fleet put in at the island they found no one alive. The island had become a desert.

All through the history of Aegina there were these alternations of abundance and ruin. At one time or another nearly every nation which seized power in the eastern Mediterranean sacked it. In its heyday, according to Aristotle, there was a slave population of 470,000. Today it has a population of 12,000. Those figures tell the terrifying story.

But as the bus wandered along the smiling valleys, there was no trace of the terror which so often visited the island. I remember a blue-domed church set in a barren field, and some young Greeks feasting like gypsies under the olive trees. It was high summer, and no rain had fallen since May, but the orchards were green and flowering. The bus left a great wake of dust which sailed into the air, as clear and crisp as the air of Athens.

The temple of Aphaia is reached through the pinewoods, lush and sweet-smelling, overlooking the Saronic Gulf. The Greek genius for finding the most perfect site for their temples was once more in evidence. There was the rolling pine-clad hill towering above the bay of St. Marina, so blue and evanescent that it resembled a quiet lake, and on this bluff stood the blaze of yellow columns like tongues of flame against the sky.

Everything we know about the ancient history of Aegina suggests an intense preoccupation with masculine virility. They were a warrior race, and they produced some of the very best athletes known to the

Greek world. They seem to have been a harsh, good-humored mer-
cantile people passionately addicted to sports, not very imaginative,
without the delicacy and cunning of the Athenians. They resembled
their virile landscape: the stern grandeur of the Aeginetan mountains
suggests a people accustomed to worship Zeus rather than Apollo.

The temple was built, as we know, to celebrate the victory at
Salamis where the Aeginetans distinguished themselves by throwing
thirty of their best ships into the battle, characteristically keeping
back part of their fleet to protect their island. Even today those
twenty-two columns suggest the thrust of victory.

The temple of Aphaia suffered the same fate as the Parthenon. It
was stripped bare of its sculptures, which were removed to decorate
a museum in Bavaria. By an odd chance they were first discovered
by a brilliant young English architect, Charles Cockerell, who traveled
out to Greece in 1810. He met Byron in Athens, and then went off to
explore Aegina. Cockerell's main concern was to draw up an accurate
plan of the famous temple. The sculptures had fallen off the pediments, and it was some time before he discovered them. Few men
have written so well about their discoveries in Greece, and he is
worth quoting at length:

> The seas hereabouts are still infested with pirates, as they al-
> ways have been. One of the workmen pointed me out the pirate
> boats off Sunium, which is one of their favorite haunts, and
> which can be seen from the temple platform. But they never
> molested us during the twenty days and nights we camped out
> there, for our party, with servants and janissary, was too strong
> to be meddled with. We got our provisions and labourers from
> the town, our fuel was the wild thyme, there were abundance of
> partridges to eat, and we bought kids from the shepherds; and
> when work was over for the day, there was a grand roasting of
> them over a blazing fire with an accompaniment of native music,
> singing and dancing. On the platform was growing a crop of
> barley, but on the actual ruins and fallen fragments of the temple
> itself no great amount of vegetable earth had collected, so that
> without very much labour we were able to find and examine
> all the stones necessary for a complete architectural analysis and
> restoration. At the end of a few days we had learned all we
> could wish to know of the construction, from the stylobate to

the tiles, and had done all we came to do.

But meanwhile a startling incident had occurred which wrought us all to the highest pitch of excitement. On the second day one of the excavators, working in the interior portico, struck on a piece of Parian marble which, as the building itself is of stone, arrested his attention. It turned out to be the head of a helmeted warrior, perfect in every feature. It lay with the face turned upwards, and as the features came out by degrees you can imagine nothing like the state of rapture and excitement to which we were wrought. Here was an altogether new interest, which set us to work with a will. Soon another head was turned up, then a leg and a foot, and finally, to make a long story short, we found under the fallen portions of the tympanum and the cornice of the eastern and western pediments no less than sixteen statues and thirteen heads, legs, arms, etc.

It was not to be expected that we should be allowed to carry away what we had found without opposition. However much people may neglect their own possessions, as soon as they see them coveted by others they begin to value them. The primates of the island came to us in a body and read a statement made by the council of the island in which they begged us to desist from our operations, for that heaven only knew what misfortunes might not fall on the island in general, and the immediately surrounding land in particular, if we continued them. Such a rubbishy pretense of superstitious fear was obviously a mere excuse to extort money, and as we felt that it was only fair that we should pay, we sent our dragoman with them to the village to treat about the sum; and meanwhile a boat which we had ordered from Athens having arrived, we embarked the marbles without delay, and sent them off to the Piraeus, and from thence they were carried off to Athens by night to avoid exciting attention.

Unfortunately for Cockerell, who hoped the sculptures would pass into the possession of the British Museum, the Turkish authorities heard about the project and seized all the sculptures. In the following year they were auctioned off at Xante. The French government and Prince Ludwig of Bavaria put in their bids, while the representative of the British Museum, who was in Greece, was carefully misled about the time and place of the sale. The highest bid came from Prince

Ludwig, who offered 10,000 sequins for the entire collection. The sculptures were removed to the Glyptothek in Munich, where they have remained ever since.

The sculptures on the temple of Aphaia are full of movement, strangely taut, so alarmingly vigorous that when you see them at Munich you wonder how the pediments could have contained them. They were closer to the statues of Olympia than those of the Parthenon. Aphaia, the protecting goddess, stood in the center; around her athletic warriors stabbed at each other, some with spears, others with short swords, all of them caught up in the agony of combat. In the corners were dying warriors. They died with clenched teeth, legs sliding convulsively along the ground, hands crisped on their swords, their heads bent in surrender. The sculptor who made these statues had seen men dying.

Only some fragments remain of the statue of Aphaia, goddess and huntress, protector of women. Like Athene she was helmeted, and like Athene too she wore a cloak of invisibility. Pausanias says the goddess came from Crete and was originally Dictynna, the half-sister of King Minos, who fell in love with her and chased her until she jumped over a cliff in despair, only to be saved by some fishing nets stretched out to dry. She was also known as Britomartis, and rather surprisingly the goddess appears in the third book of Spenser's *Faerie Queene*, "wherein is contained the Legend of Britomartis or of Chastity."

The masterpiece among these sculptures is a kneeling warrior who wears a helmet made of the muzzle of a lion and a coat armored with plaques of iron. He kneels, stretching his bow, and there is the faintest of archaic smiles on his lips. He has the look of a god, and may be Hercules. Of all the surviving figures he alone has the look of calm majesty, of quivering delight in life.

The subtle features of the young Hercules are not easily forgotten. He bears himself with wide-eyed dignity and sovereign ease, remote from the conflict while yet a part of it. Though kneeling, he has the commanding aspect of the Peirithoös at Olympia. He does not have to shoot the arrow. He is of those who stay the battle by his mere presence.

Seeing this young Aeginetan, we know all we need to know about the young athletes of the island, for whom Pindar wrote at least eleven of his odes. He showed a special gentleness and affection to the Aeginetans. Here he is celebrating the victory of the young Deinias, who had recently lost his father, also a runner:

> In honor of the beloved city and her citizens
> I throw my arms around the hallowed knees of Aiakos, bearing
> This Lydian veil embroidered with resounding song,
> So that Deinias may be remembered for his race at Nemea,
> And so that Megas too may be remembered.
> Triumph remains longer among men
> When it comes from the hands of a God.
>
> Glory also increaseth like the vines'
> Young green tendrils, and riseth among men
> Who are virtuous and wise into the clear skies.
> For various are the uses of friendship,
> And nothing is so hard to grasp, but joy
> Clamours after truth and the clear-lidded eyes.
> O Megas, I cannot bring you back to life:
> Only despair awaits those who would attempt the feat.
> But now, even now I raise up in your city
> This marble column of the Muses to honor
> The day when you run races, and now
> The day of your son.

When Pindar praised the Syracusans, he embroidered his odes with so much jewelry that almost they collapse under the weight of splendor. When he speaks of the Aeginetans, he is more forthright. He loves them for their defense of strangers, their justice, their boldness in battle, their courage in adversity. For him Aegina was an island which "kept glory perfect from the beginning." He cannot altogether escape from the splendor of his imagery, for he promises them a necklace of the Muses fashioned of "white ivory and gold inlaid and coral of the lily flower gathered beneath the ocean dew."

The greatest of his odes was written in honor of the young Aeginetan Aristomenes who won the wrestling match at Delphi in 446 B.C. There is only a brief glimpse of the boy, but the poet dwells longingly on the island, celebrating it above all other islands. Since

Coin from Elis, showing head of Zeus by Phidias, c. 363 B.C.

Hero of Artemision

Caryatids on Erechtheion

The Erechtheion

Delphi

Sounion

The Acropolis

Socrates from Greek original of fourth century B.C.

he is writing about a victory at the Pythian games, he demands a special blessing from Apollo, who gives brightness to men:

He who has won some new splendor
Rides on the air,
Borne upward on the wings of his human vigor
In a fierce pride of hope, rejoicing
In no desire for wealth, enjoying
For a brief space the exaltation of glory,
Until at last he falls to the earth
Shattered by the beckoning doom.

We are things of a day. What are we? What are we not? The shadow of
    a dream.
We are all shadows, but when the shining comes from the hands of the
    God,
Then the heavenly light falls on men, and life is all sweetness.

In the brief fifty-year history of Greece in her utmost splendor, Aegina has a special place. That temple of Aphaia hidden among the pines showed the beginning of Greek supremacy in art, and that kneeling archer is the forerunner of all the heroic sculptures at Olympia and on the Parthenon.

X ATHENS

Very often the traveler in Athens finds himself asking inconvenient questions. Walking under that fantastically deep blue sky, he sometimes has to remind himself that he is still in Europe. Athens is oriental. It wears the colors of the Orient, and the people have the ripeness and luxuriance of the Orient. The women often wear veils, as they do in Persia. They walk slowly and gracefully, and no one hurries. The cafés are full of men repeating the wildest and most improbable gossip. It might be Isfahan or Tabriz. Is this, the traveler asks himself, the cradle of western civilization? What is all the fuss about?

We assume too readily that western civilization must have its origin in a western city, but Greece never belonged to the West. She was always at the crossroads, closer in spirit to Persia than to Rome. Her task was to impose order and harmony on the fierce luxuriance of the East and to weave a net of logic over the violent fantasies that came out of Asia. Her originality lay in being calm, but she was never calm for long. There were times when Dionysus seemed to triumph over Apollo. Christ and Apollo do not reign unchallenged.

Everywhere you go in Athens you meet the Orient. It is not only the brilliance of the sky and the waving palm trees, and it has little to do with the endless years of Turkish occupation. It is in the quick faces of the Athenians, in the alert gleam in their eyes, in their nervous gestures—they share with the Persians the habit of telling beads to prevent themselves from exploding. Sitting in the cafés or in the pleasant restaurants of Plaka, otherwise impeccable businessmen tell

115

atrocious stories about their friends in a language admirably formed for the delivery of innuendoes and gentle obscenities. There is nothing new in this. In the time of Pericles there was a good deal of dangerous gossip. It was said that Pericles accepted peacocks on behalf of his mistresses, and the queer shape of his head came about because ———. The Greeks, and especially the Athenians, have mastered the art of talking without words. They have an infinity of gestures and sudden shakes of the head. We remember how Achilles in the *Iliad* "signalled to Patroclus with his eyebrows to make a bed for Phoenix." It has become more complicated now, but the essentials have not changed.

We are continually being told that the Greeks of today are unrelated to the ancient Greeks. How, we are asked, could a nation maintain its purity over three thousand years, after continual invasions? No, the Greeks of our day are Turks, Levantines, Syrians, Alexandrians, a hodgepodge of all the races of the Near East. Unfortunately for the enemies of Greece, the theory will not hold up. Everywhere you go in Greece you come upon the classic features. I have seen a peasant standing in a field near Eleutherae who might have sat for a portrait of Apollo. There are girls in Athens who look as though they had stepped down from the Porch of the Maidens. One day, while I was walking around Plaka, a horde of schoolboys came roaring out of a street: I had seen the same features only a few minutes before on the Parthenon frieze which is shown round all the walls of the Acropolis Museum.

The astonishing thing is how little the Greeks have changed. I suspect that the ancestors of the modern Greeks were as charming and ruthless, as nervous and excitable as their descendants; and I know why so many strings of beads have been found in ancient graves.

THE PARTHENON

There are mysteries about the Parthenon which no one has ever solved. I do not mean the mysteries of *entasis* and the bending of the columns, and exactly how they worshiped Athene, and whether the

Parthenon frieze can be reconciled with the Panathenaic procession, and all those other problems which are the delight of scholars and architects. The real mystery lies elsewhere. Why is it that of all the buildings in the world this one alone, though ruined and damaged beyond repair, speaks with a clear unhurried voice of its own perfection?

There are only a handful of authentically great buildings left in the world. In their different ways Santa Sophia in Constantinople, the Temple of Heaven in Peking, the Mosque of Sheikh Lutfullah in Isfahan, the Taj Mahal in Agra and the Dome of the Rock in Jerusalem have achieved that perfection which is reserved only for the highest works of art, but none of them approach the perfect dignity of the Parthenon, that utmost grandeur. There is something almost insolent in the way the Parthenon says quietly: "I have been worn to the bone, but I am the most living of all things."

Insolent it is, as it rides on the purple rock, like a ship with all its sails flying: a very weather-beaten ship with spars and sails torn to tatters, the deck staved in, the planking gone, nothing left except the bare ribs. Once it was drenched with color: with blue and scarlet and gold. Once it contained heaps of treasure from all over the Greek world and an elaborate statue of Athene which reached to the roof, and bearded priests in white garments attended the goddess. What is left—those honey-colored pillars, the drums and the cornices—is, we tell ourselves, more splendid than anything the Greeks ever saw, for time and an explosion of gunpowder have removed the embroidery and shown us the temple in its perfect nakedness. Today we see the Parthenon very nearly as the Greeks saw it when it was being built, when Ictinus was superintending the design and Phidias was carving the sculptures. We see it as it was about 440 B.C., twenty-four hundred years ago.

This is one of the miracles among many miracles: that we can look upon a thing so old in all its freshness. It is still being built, still to be completed, but time has preserved it in a moment of exquisite purity, the bud opening, not yet in flower. Nothing quite like this has happened to any of the great surviving buildings in the world. The Taj Mahal and Santa Sophia are only too abundantly decorated.

Only to the Parthenon was it given to survive after innumerable mis-adventures in its virgin splendor.

That year—440 B.C.—when the Parthenon was only half completed, and there was no roof, no pediment, and no frieze, Sophocles brought out the *Antigone*, a play which gave the Athenians so much happiness that they appointed him one of the ten *strategi* in the war against Samos: for the only time in history a great poet received a military command. In the *Antigone* Sophocles announced the theme which was to become the faith by which the Athenians lived their dangerous lives:

> *Many marvels there are,*
> *But none so marvellous as Man.*

Man indeed had become the master of the world, stepping out of the darkness of dreams into sunlight, full, rounded and complete, as we see him in the statues of Alcamenes which were produced only a few years earlier. Never again was man to assume quite that super-human appearance; never again was he to exult so joyously in his powers. There was no sense of guilt; the *Phaedo* was a long way away; the Beatitudes were still to come. In time the Hellenistic sculptors would smooth the contours and give more prominence to the intricate draperies than to the firm flesh. But at this particular moment in the world's history, on an early morning in a spring day of 440 B.C., the human spirit was reaching out to one of those rare pinnacles of achievement, and having reached this summit it seemed to know there remained only the long downward path, the descent into nightmare again.

The Greeks knew; and they did not know. They walked about the streets of Athens, hardly realizing that a miracle had happened. In the memory of men still living Athens had been put to the torch by the Persians. The whole Acropolis had been burned down, and even the sacred olive tree was burned to the roots, though it was observed that a long new shoot sprang up the next day. The promise of the olive tree was being fulfilled. A new vigor, a new certainty walked by their side.

Pericles had given orders for the reconstruction of the Parthenon, and all the rubble of the Acropolis, all those heaps of broken sandstone pillars, blackened and reddened by fire, all those statues, including the statue of Athene herself which had fallen to the earth during the fire, were cleared away or buried in the places on the Acropolis where there were dips and hollows, so that the whole platform was smoothed over; and then the general plan was carefully outlined. The Propylaea, forming the great entrance gates, and the Erechtheion, which would contain the *xoanon,* the sacred image of Athene, were to come later. Meanwhile thousands of workmen were employed to cut stone, build roads, splice ropes, fell forests and construct the ships which would bring rare woods and marble from afar. Carpenters, masons, braziers, goldsmiths, painters, turners, iron-founders and even leather-cutters were pressed into service; and the road between Athens and the quarries of Penteli was crushed into deep ruts and ravaged by winter rains. Nearly all of Athens was set to work on the building of the Parthenon so that, in the words of Pericles, "the heart may be warmed and the eye delighted forever."

It was a time when the greatest intelligences ever produced by Athens were living and walking about the city, many of them coming or about to come into their maturity. Just the year before Euripides had gained the first prize. He was forty, a heavy-set, thickly bearded man weighed down with a raw melancholy that he could never quite overcome. Socrates was thirty, and beginning his gay criticism of all accepted codes. Thucydides was the same age as Socrates, and he was perhaps already preparing his great history, though the Peloponnesian war was to come later, bringing an end to the glory of Periclean Athens. Sophocles was forty-five, and was to live for another half century. He was about the same age as Herodotus, who was already known as "the historian," as though another comparable historian was unthinkable. Phidias was fifty, and Polyclitus perhaps twenty years older. It was as though all the talents in the world had congregated in the city of Athens, which was hardly a city at all, but a huddle of small low buildings at the foot of the Acropolis. Most of the inhabitants lived in the Ceramicus, which Thucydides called "our most beautiful suburb." But the town was unprepossessing, with very little to be said in its favor. Dicaearchus, a disciple of Aristotle, described it as "dusty and ill-supplied with water, wretchedly laid out on account of its antiquity, while the majority of the houses are mean, and very few good. A stranger at first sight might well doubt that this is Athens."

The Athenians never succeeded in building a beautiful city. To this day it remains curiously ramshackle, with few vantage points pleasing to the eye. They built no great colonnaded avenues like those at Antioch and Alexandria; there were no lavishly ornamented parks and hanging gardens like those at Babylon; though they invented town planning and spoke endlessly of the city, the *polis*, they made no plans for Athens, and for them the city meant "our people within the walls." Because they attached more importance to people than to their living quarters, and more importance to the gods than to the people, they built their ideal city on the Acropolis for all to look at. They built a palace for the gods and were content to live in its shadow in whatever hovels they could find.

We think of the Acropolis as the private garden of grey-eyed Athene, whose immense statue guarded the approaches to the sacred precincts, but in fact it was peopled by all the gods of Greece. Artemis had her altar there; so did Apollo; and there was a temple for Asclepius on the slopes. There were altars to the legendary Cecrops, who founded the city, and his beautiful daughter Pandrosus, formed of the morning dew. The mysterious Erechtheus, father of Cecrops, had his own dwelling place; and when the Romans conquered Greece, there was even an altar for Augustus Caesar. Athene herself was worshiped under all her many and conflicting aspects. There was Athene the Warrior, shaking her spear; there was Athene the Companion, almost the lover; there was Athene of the Household, presiding over the young weavers, "the goddess of all things fair and temperately fashioned," who gazed down at her charges with maternal solicitude; there was Athene the Virgin, immaculate and all-powerful, resolute to protect her city. There was also, and most unexpectedly, Athene the Goddess of Love, who uttered the charms which brought forth fertility in women. Once a year her priestesses went on a solemn pilgrimage, bearing on their heads mysterious baskets. In these baskets were sharp knives.

These priestesses are represented in the porch of the Erechtheion. As they stand there in stately magnificence, they have the air of being spectators of the Parthenon. In fact they were the armed guardians of the most sacred and dangerous temple in Athens.

The Erechtheion is a very mysterious place indeed. It was here, and not in the Parthenon, that the sacred robe of Athene, the *peplos*, was preserved. Here, too, was the ancient wooden image, the *xoanon*, of the goddess, and her olive tree. Here was the golden lamp which was never allowed to go out, and the bronze palm tree through which the smoke of the lamp was led up to a hole in the roof. It was on that ground that Athene contended with Poseidon in that duel which was commemorated on the pediment of the Parthenon. The entire Acropolis was sacred, but those few square feet of rock were the most sacred of all.

Athene won her enduring victory, but she was in no mood for vengeance. She pardoned her adversary and permitted him to have an altar in the Erechtheion, and there were other altars to Erechtheus, his still more legendary half-brother Butus, and to Hephaestus, the god of fire. The marks left by Poseidon's trident were allowed to remain, and a part of the roof was left open to show the path of the flaming trident as it came to earth on the Acropolis, and the salt well which was sacred to him was also shown. Poseidon, defeated, was permitted to retain all his honors. Indeed, Athene seems to have given him pride of place on the Parthenon pediment, for Carrey's drawing shows Poseidon in all his magnificence as he leans a little backward, hurling his trident at her. Yet she no longer has any cause to fear him; she is the undisputed mistress of her temple; and though the Erechtheion was named after a god of the most remote antiquity, she is herself the queen of the temple.

The Erechtheion was a repository of the most ancient gods, who lived in an uneasy alliance with one another. She did not fear these gods, though they had once reigned supreme over Athens and were therefore capable of desperate stratagems to regain their former power. They belonged to the ancient barbaric darkness; Athene belonged to the light. Out of her mercy she provided them with a share of her royal dwelling.

The Parthenon is wholly masculine; the Erechtheion is wholly feminine. It has the waywardness, the faintly sinister gracefulness, the delight in adorning herself of a truly beautiful woman. It is a very delicate temple, rich with honeysuckle ornamentation and the supple flutings of the Ionic columns. The same ornamental sunflowers which decorate the palaces of the Persian kings at Persepolis are carved beside the portals, and there is more than a hint of Persian influence. The tides of Asia sweep up to the Acropolis: even the Parthenon itself betrays an Ionian influence. In the Doric temple the ratio between front and sides is 1:2. In the Parthenon it follows the Ionian ratio of 2:3.

The Parthenon then represents Athene in her masculine aspects as goddess of war, defender of the city, the champion of the clear-sighted intelligence. There is no hint of severity in the Erechtheion. Here she wears her robes, having put armor away, and cultivates her olive trees, and watches over the dead and dying gods of the past. Those eastern waves which break against the cliffs of the Acropolis produced two temples of amazing complexity, one which seems to stride forward with relentless power, while the other holds back. One is a great army on the march, the other is a group of maidens in a palace. With daring and extreme refinement of taste the Greeks were able to hold the two temples in a trembling balance.

They accomplished this miraculous feat at a time of desperate peril, about the year 409 B.C., at the height of the Peloponnesian War, for the Erechtheion is very late and comes as the last superb achievement of Greek architecture. It seems to have been designed with the terrible lucidity which comes only at moments of great danger.

"The Athenians," says the Corinthian ambassador in Thucydides, "are always innovators quick to form resolutions and quick to carry them out. Their daring outruns their resources, and they will always take risks against their better judgment, but they remain calm in times of danger."

Socrates still haunts Athens. Wrapped in a long woolen cloak he wanders beside the Ilissus in the company of his disciples—stern Plato with his quick and blinding smiles, rosy-cheeked Agathon, and thin dark-faced Chaerophon, who always looked half-starved and was perhaps the closest of all. If we can trust the statue in the British Museum, Socrates walked with elegance and grace, and in spite of the snub nose and the strange light which sometimes shone in his eyes there was nothing ugly in his appearance. He had a curious way of looking at his questioners, as though he were taunting them, half in mockery and half in kindness. He had a rich crackling laugh. He was strong as an ox, and had been known to stand for long hours in meditation in the snow. His father was a stone cutter, and he had inherited his father's skill.

So much one knows, and though he haunts Athens and sometimes it is possible to believe that he is physically present in the city, I had not thought that anything of him survived outside the writings of those who knew him. It never occurred to me that Flaubert may have touched one of his sculptures.

Flaubert came to Athens in the winter of 1850 on his return from a visit to the Near East. He was intensely excited by Greece, though he detested Greek officials and he was especially displeased by the sight of Queen Amalie riding through the streets. "She has rabbit's eyes, and too yellow eyebrows," he wrote. "She eats six meals a day, and has no lover." He did not altogether approve of the Parthenon: "It is the color of brick, and in some places the color of bitumen and ink. Falcons and ravens perch on the broken columns; and while the wind whispers through the temple, the goats wander freely among the broken debris of white marble. Here and there you come upon a heap of bones in a hollow of the earth, left over from the wars."

He was excited beyond measure by his discovery of a torso lying among the ruins, where it had fallen. It was not greatly damaged. One breast was covered with a veil, the other was uncovered. The entire torso from the neck to the waist lay there, and he could not take his eyes away. He fondled it in a fury of admiration. He would have taken it back to France with him if it was not so heavy.

"What a breast this is!" he wrote. "So full, so rich—round like an apple! It is quite separated from the other breast, and is very heavy in the hand. A breast which has known fecund maternities and those delights of love for which men die! Rain and sun have turned the white marble yellow. There is a vivid color in it, and that is why it resembles flesh, and is so quiet, and so noble.

"Almost you have the feeling that this torso can breathe, and the chest will expand. How charmingly she wears the simple folds of her draperies. It would be so easy to throw oneself weeping on this woman! I would have thrown myself at her feet with my hands folded in prayer! Standing before her, I felt the beauty of the expression: 'Stupet acris.' A moment more, and I would have started praying!"

Flaubert found the torso close to the place where, according to Pausanias, stood the Hermes and the Graces sculpted by "Socrates, the son of Sophroniscus, who was said by the Pythia to be the wisest of men." I could find no trace of the torso either in the Acropolis Museum or in the National Museum, but it may still be in existence. Somewhere there may still be the torso of one of the Graces, who were the handmaidens of Apollo, carved by Socrates and fondled by Flaubert.

THE HERO OF ARTEMISION

He stands in one of the wings of the National Gallery of Athens in all the plenitude of his power, the perfect image of man at the height of human glory. Once his eyes were filled with little pieces of colored glass and onyx, but now they are empty sockets. This blind man gives the impression of seeing more and further than any statue ever created.

He stands there striding forward with his arms outflung, quivering with vitality, an invisible spear poised in his right hand, and though the body is in movement and a relentless battle is about to be fought, the face with the long jutting beard is curiously detached, impassive, godlike. Imagine the Peirithoös at Olympia grown to maturity— imagine him raising the other arm and striding out toward the conquest of new worlds, filling all the space around him with his own power, and you have an approximation of this bronze statue which seems to have been dipped in gold, so cleverly has it been cleaned and put together from the fragments salvaged in 1928 from a depth of twenty fathoms off Cape Artemision, on the northeast coast of Euboea, by fishermen who were surprised to find in their nets the limbs of a godlike hero.

Here is the crowning glory of Greek art: beyond this it was not possible to go. Just as the Peirithoös shows the emergence of the Western consciousness, so this statue from Artemision shows the same consciousness in its most commanding aspect. Here is man vividly alive, capable of the utmost daring, wide-eyed and in perfect control, endowed with so much grace, so much physical beauty and so much intelligence that almost he escapes from being man and becomes a god. The statue embodies whatever of divinity may be incarnated in human form.

Who is he? No one knows for certain. It has been suggested that the statue represents Zeus the Thunderer, about to hurl his lightning, but Zeus was never represented naked or with a body of such youthful beauty. It is possible that it represents Poseidon, who together with Athene dominated the western pediment of the Parthenon. Most of the sculptures on the pediment were still standing in 1674 and in that year an artist attached to the retinue of the French ambassador to the Sublime Porte made a drawing of the pediment, which shows Poseidon naked, his legs stretched wide apart, his body bent over a little as he is about to hurl his trident. But the Greek artist made many statues of heroes, setting them up on the Acropolis and many other public places. It may be Poseidon; it may be Hercules, or even Apollo, or an unknown hero. What is certain is that the statue represents the Greek conception of heroism and nobility of mind in its utmost extent.

Everything about the statue betrays the hand of a recognizable master. Here and there among the great fragments from the Parthenon now in the British Museum we can recognize the authentic works of Phidias by their alertness, their almost casual grace, their wonderfully rich and flowing modeling. The muscles are not reproduced with anatomical accuracy, but with an imagined clarity. The sculptured bodies represent perfectly developed men rather than athletes; there is a hint of austerity in them. The horse of Selene and the Theseus on the east pediment of the Parthenon are manifestly by the same hand; they reflect each other; and both in turn illustrate the hero from Artemision. The clean lines mount like waves and explode in decorative wave caps. The intricate beard and hair of the hero from Artemision express his character as abstract design, but they also form in abstract terms a release from all the pent-up energy in the figure. On that figure, in that stance, a beardless head would be an impertinence. The very energy of the beard fills out the character of the hero: those waves of fire pushing relentlessly forward.

One should beware of imagining the Greeks of the classical age as men possessed of an inner calm, that calm which is suggested by the proportions of the Parthenon or by the face of the youth at Olympia who raises his arm in a gesture of sovereign authority. On the contrary they maintained their composure only with the greatest difficulty, seething with a nervous violence. They were untamable creatures of instinct, loving the flesh. A wild sap flowed through them, and they were incapable of concealing their desires. For them reason was a new-found weapon, so bright and gleaming that it blinded them, and they used it cautiously, with a kind of reluctance, preferring like Socrates to rely on their daimons than upon the processes of the mind.

So it is with the hero of Artemision. He is all that is majestic, conscious of his own dignity, aware of everything that happens around him. He knows exactly who he is, where he is, what he is doing. One foot is firmly planted on the ground, and he weighs heavily on the earth, being of the earth, earthy. But from the feet upward there moves a violent flame, almost visible as it pours over the swelling thighs and across the rippling torso and then leaps along the arms.

Almost he is consumed in the flame. The sculptor has achieved what one would have thought to be impossible—he has found the exact balance between the earthiness of man and the flame which lifts him up to heaven and God. In that tension the hero exists in perfect equipoise. But when the equipoise is broken, when the spear or trident is hurled, what then? Look carefully on that face, which bears within it more than a hint of the archaic. Surely there will come from him a barbaric cry of triumph.

Admiring the texture and the extraordinary power contained in the bronze, one forgets that this is a man or a divinity determined to kill. He might be Achilles, "advancing like a great mountain" against the doomed Trojans. He is no athlete throwing some harmless disc across the playing field. His purposes are those of destruction, weapon poised, one hand pointing rigidly at the mark. Nothing in the world or above the world will deflect him from his fatal purpose. It is perturbing that the supreme work of ancient times should show man at his most godlike and most deadly, but it is perhaps inevitable.

When the young Bettina von Arnim went to visit the aging poet Friedrich Hölderlin, she listened quietly while he poured out a stream of strange utterances derived from his long association with Greek poetry. Among them were the words: "Murder flows from the divine."

Yet of all things created in the Western world this murderer is the most perfect representation of man. Beside him Michelangelo's *David* is scarcely more than a fleshly youth, and Cellini's *Perseus* is an actor in a commonplace charade. All are murderers. It seems to be one of the fatal flaws of Western consciousness that it can only represent power in terms of murderers and their victims. Already the hero of Artemision wears the lineaments of guilt.

Pride is there, and vast ambitions, and the splendor which has nothing to do with royal garments and great possessions, but more important than any of these is his elementary power and beauty. All that is superfluous has been strenuously excluded. He wears his nakedness like a robe, but it is an absolute nakedness. Relentless and pitiless, he stands at that point in Athenian history which is the pinnacle of achievement, being himself the measure by which all Athenian art must be measured. He says nothing, but everything about him proclaims his violent joy in living.

Never again was there to be a statue comparable to this. Henceforward there could only be the downhill path, which would end with the *Hermes* of Praxiteles and the delicate embroideries of the Hellenistic artists. About the year 440 B.C., when this statue was made, the flame burned brightest. Ever since it has been gradually dying out.

AMPHARETE

Sometimes a small and unimportant object will catch the eye and because of some unexpected beauty it becomes intolerably precious. Sometimes the famous paintings pall, and in some unexpected corner of a gallery, on a painting which has almost nothing to commend it, there can be found a detail, a splash of color, a texture which is alarmingly filled with significance. I remember at Delphi some small ivory toys representing dancers, all of them with archaic smiles on their white faces, but these smiles were somehow belied by the vigor of their limbs. They lay in a glass case. They were broken. Some had clipped wings, others had holes punched through them, and there were arms, legs and heads scattered in profusion. Hardly one was more than two inches high, but what life flowed through those ivory veins, and how passionately they continued their three-thousand-year-old dance!

I remember at the same museum the head of a young scholar, lightly bearded, a face of extraordinary intelligence, such a face as one might imagine belonging to a contemplative descendant of the Peirithoös of Olympia, full of authority and grace, but self-doubt and self-indifference had crept in, and there was more than a hint of brooding austerity in those heavily lidded eyes and in the casual sweetness of the smile: so men smile when they know they are dying.

Portrait: Hellenistic Epoch reads the inscription, which is almost certainly inaccurate, for there is a fullness of expression which belongs to an earlier age; and you leave the statue and make your way inevitably to the green charioteer, who is not a charioteer, but there is no escaping this young philosopher, who haunts you as the *Mona Lisa* haunts you, and for the same reason: he is speaking, saying something which he desperately wants you to hear, but the voice is drowned in the clamor of the ages. The charioteer is silent and self-contained within his beauty, but this young scholar insists on speaking. It is a shattering experience to stand beside him and hear nothing at all.

Toys from Knossos, a hank of hair from an Egyptian princess who died five thousand years ago, a chipped face of a girl who died in Byzantium at the time of Justinian, a gold ribbon which once bound the hair of an athlete at the Pythian games—those are things which sometimes have more meaning for us than the most superb statues, the most magnificent buildings. The small statue of Socrates hidden away behind a glass case in a corner of the British Museum tells us more about how Socrates walked about Athens than volumes of commentary. There are trinkets found in the grave of an Athenian girl which tell us more about life in the time of Pericles than all the speeches of the rulers of the city. The small things tell us most; for the smallest griefs and the smallest joys are the most enduring.

In the museum at Athens there is a grave stele which can be dated to the middle of the fifth century B.C. It is a relief of a woman holding a child in her arms, and though it is only the thickness of a fingernail, worn and roughened by winds, rain and frost, yet every detail can still be seen clearly. Inscribed in classic Greek letters below the relief are the words:

> My daughter's dear child I hold upon my lap, as once in ancient days I held him, when we looked with loving eyes on the sun. Now the child is dead, and I, Ampharete, who held him, am also dead.

All the Greeks' hunger for life, their lucidity, their dazed acceptance of death with no hope of an afterlife, even their quietness and nobility, are on that worn stone.

XI S O U N I O N

In the blue dusk of the lower air the fishing boats swept past Helen's island, where she first gave herself to Paris, and somewhere in the gathering darkness of the hills we thought we could make out the fretted galleries of Laurion, where slaves once burrowed into the earth for silver. Across the sea lay the hoary mountains of the Argolid.

Dusk—the blue and purple dusk—is the best time for Sounion. Then those chaste and pure white columns are no longer so intimidating. By day they look as though they were whitewashed, without character. But at dusk and at sunrise color floods over them. I have seen them frosty pink at dawn, and there are evenings when they are golden. They are actors taking on the colors of their surroundings.

I have been to Sounion often, and always with a faint sense of disappointment. Of all Greek temples it is the most artful, the most delicate. It suggests ormolu clocks and lace embroidery. The temple was built many years after the Parthenon, when the Greek genius for combining solidity and vigor was already waning, when they were exhausted with their fierce explosions of energy. One imagines the architect was pleased with himself. He was careful to choose a site at exactly the right distance from the marble cliffs; the columns are exactly the right height, they point in exactly the right direction. The temple was, of course, a closed space invading the skyline, and so we have an advantage over the ancient Greeks: those twelve slender columns decorate the headland more artfully than any temple. So the Chinese out of their ancient wisdom placed pagodas on the barren hills and somehow gave life to them.

The temple of Athene at Sounion belongs to the decorator's art, at an infinite remove from the Parthenon. Those columns were put there for effect. How charming they are in their chocolate-box way—how charming, and also how repetitive! Two columns would be enough. Even one column might do the work of twelve. Twelve columns! It is almost too much!

But in the late evening, at dusk, when the hills turn purple and the sea thickens to blackness, these lean and athletic columns, weathered by the winds of more than twenty centuries, seem to possess a quivering life of their own as they catch the last glimmerings of sunset. The decorator never guessed how beautiful they would become for a few minutes each day.

No ghosts and no legends attach to Sounion. Pausanias began his travels through Greece here, but he could find nothing at all to say about it except that an obscure ship's captain returning from the Trojan wars died and was buried here. More legends and innumerable ghosts haunt the Laurion mines nearby, where the slaves lived in unspeakable squalor to provide wealth for Athens. Almost the only historical record concerning the temple describes how it had to be garrisoned during the Peloponnesian War against the slaves who were always escaping from the mines.

The Greeks have very sensibly built a restaurant within sight of the columns, but far enough away so that you can take in the whole of the soaring headland. Sitting there, drinking ouzo and happily befuddled, you wait for the moonrise. But when the moon strikes the columns the artifice becomes transparent. Too slender to suggest power, too delicate to dominate the headland, the ghostly columns seem to have been painted neatly on a backdrop.

Poor Sounion! The tourists invade the ruined temple even more resolutely than they invade the Parthenon, and they stay longer, so that it is almost impossible to photograph it. They scrawl their names on the columns as close as possible to the deeply cut signature of Byron, who must have spent half a day with chisel and mallet cutting his reprehensible signature into the rock. They gape and chatter. Someone has told them that Sounion is one of the masterpieces of Greek art. Unhappily they are mistaken: much of the temple is a modern reconstruction, and it betrays nearly all the characteristics of Greek art at its worst.

Still, there are compensations. The drive from Athens along the seacoast is always pleasant. It is especially pleasant to make the journey by night, when the moon is low and the mysterious landscape is touched with silver. In this light the grey and withered olive trees acquire a strangely human quality. They become faces, the hair of old women, old men writhing in agony. I remember traveling late one night along the deserted road. It was very dark, and a huge sadness weighed on Attica. There was only the long silent road, and the ghostly olive trees. Suddenly, five miles from Phaleron, the automobile screamed to a stop. There, before us, completely unconcerned, were two white oxen with delicately curving horns and quivering flanks glowing in the beams of the headlights. They were majestic as they stood there, so quiet and peaceful and unmoved, their flanks the purest white and their eyes silver.

We switched off the headlights. Then very gently, with the utmost grace, the oxen tossed their heads and ambled into the dark.

XII   D A P H N I

In the days when the pilgrims streamed along the sacred way to Eleusis, they would pause on the brow of a hill about seven miles from Athens and make offerings at the temple of Apollo. It was a small white temple of gleaming Pentelic marble with delicate Ionic columns, and it contained images of Demeter and Athene as well as Apollo. It was known as the temple of Apollo of the Laurels.

For perhaps a thousand years this temple remained beside the road, only to be destroyed by the Goths in A.D. 395. Justinian rebuilt it, using the fallen material to make one of those small fortified churches which guarded the approaches to Athens. About the year 1025 a Byzantine Emperor, perhaps Basil II, "the slayer of the Bulgars," completely renovated the church and gave it its present form. Toward the end of the century the mosaics which decorate the interior were put up, and for just over a hundred years they were permitted to stand there in all their glory in beauty. When the Franks invaded Attica in 1205 they expelled the Byzantine priests and invited the Cistercians to occupy the church. The Dukes of Athens were sometimes buried there, and the Cistercian monks added to the Orthodox church a typical cloister. It was known as the monastery of Dalfinet.

The mosaics were permitted to remain throughout the Frankish occupation, though the Cistercians probably covered them with plaster. Well-aimed Frankish bolts have been found in the eyes of the great Pantocrator who stares down from the dome. But there was very little vandalism. To the Dukes of Athens, as to the Byzantine Emperors, Daphni remained a place of sanctity. When the Catalans conquered Attica, they too were buried there. Daphni ceased to be the burial place of the rulers of Athens only when Attica passed into the hands of the Florentine banking family of Acciajuoli. The Florentines preferred to be buried on the Parthenon.

There is a tradition that Dona Chiara Acciajuoli, the last Duchess of Athens, married after her husband's death a young Venetian, Bartolomeo Contarini, to the annoyance of her nephew, Franco Acciajuoli, who hoped to inherit the dukedom. Franco made the journey to Constantinople to complain to Sultan Mahomet II, who was a little amused. He could not understand why Franco felt himself threatened by a woman. "Power comes to him who holds it," said the Sultan. "Return to Athens and see whether you are strong enough to remove her." Franco returned to Athens. He caught up with the Duchess Chiara while she was praying on the tombs of the dead Frankish rulers at Daphni, and strangled her with his own hands. A few years later the Sultan's army conquered Athens. The Sultan sent a message: "Strangle Franco." At the end of the nineteenth century a French consul wandering in the streets of Athens met a donkey-man with blue eyes and fair hair, and asked him his name. "My name is Acciajuoli," the donkey-man replied, and went on his way.

Greece became a province of the Turkish empire. The Turks permitted Orthodox worship, but they occupied the church at Daphni as a command post because it dominated the highway from Athens. Once the garrison officer gave orders for a huge fire to be lit in the church: he hoped to melt down the gold mosaics. In the sixteenth century the monks were permitted to return, but the church never recovered its former glory. It was raided by pirates, and was already in ruins when the Greeks fighting for their independence in 1821 used it as a guardpost. When the War of Independence was won, the ruined church was reconsecrated. It was known as the church of the All-Holy Virgin of the Golden Laurels.

There are no more golden laurels, but the pines keep the air fresh and pure. Apollo has not entirely vanished, for one of the Ionic columns of his temple, of incomparable grace and beauty, is built into it. It seems from outside to be a very small church with a red dome rising above the sun-warmed brick. Inside it seems to be as high as heaven.

I used to think the Cappella Palatina at Palermo was the loveliest single building in the world, worthy of the occupation of God. I have seen it during a wedding when all the candles were lit, when the mosaics on the wall and on the ceiling glittered with unearthly splendor, while the choristers chanted and the priests intoned the nuptial mass. Daphni—without priests, without candles, with only a few pathetic remnants of the mosaics which once covered its walls— is still lovelier.

On the arch of the conch at Daphni there was once an inscription in enamel letters on gold reading: "The glory of this latter house shall be greater than the former, saith the Lord of Hosts." The words suggest a deliberate attempt to create a house of unparalleled splendor, rivaling the temple of Solomon.

They succeeded beyond all expectation. Neither in Constantinople nor in Venice are there mosaics equal to these. The mosaics on the walls depict the story of Jesus as though his life were bathed in an eternal springtime. It is a world glowing with the colors of jewels, very bright, very clear. The artists have gone back to the ancient classical models. The mosaic murals, more than sixty in all, follow the traditional pattern which can be seen at Monreale, but the hieratic stiffness has gone. These people live and breathe; the air flows round them; they are quick and luminously absorbed in the scene around them. The Angel of the Annunciation wears a classic countenance, and his garments are folded in classic folds as he floats against a sky of gold, but there is not the least trace of stiffness in him; he is all eagerness and gentleness as he raises his hand in blessing. His blue and rose-red wings are no impediment. He carries a staff, and might be a young Athenian philosopher, like one of those who surrounded Socrates, on holiday.

On a nearby shell there is depicted the Nativity. Mary lies beside the cradle in her blue and star-studded gown, but her features are those of Athene. Blue-haired Joseph looks on beside an olive tree, and the shepherds gape, tugging at their beards, as they must have gaped when Poseidon made war on the goddess-queen of Athens. The shepherds peer at the miracle with the look of incredulous spectators, but the angels watch with gestures of infinite grace.

The thousands of small tesserae forming these figures were cut from the same sources which produced the ancient Greek temples and sculptures. White marble from Penteli, blue from Hymettus, black from Eleusis and brilliant white-silver from Naxos. The golden cubes were made by baking gold foil in glass, and the rich blue cubes come from the same blue dyes which are seen on Persian mosques. Persian elegance, classic form and Christian feeling are somehow combined to produce an overwhelming perfection.

At least three artists worked on the mosaics. There is the artist who worked on the Pantocrator on the dome and the shaggy, deeply troubled John the Baptist who points toward the Saviour; there is the artist who composed the severe portraits of the prophets and saints on the arches and vaults; finally there is the artist, of almost terrifying brilliance, who composed the Nativity, the Baptism, the Crucifixion and all the other scenes in the life of Christ. All are masterly. All are instinct with life. All shine with a white and gold radiance.

In the Baptism the naked body of Christ is seen in the waters of the Jordan, while the dove and the rays of God fall from heaven and John blesses him from the bank. They are real rays and a real dove, and the waters are trembling and throwing off sparks of light. The dove is prancing in mid-air with an expression of exquisite joy almost too great to be borne. Two angels wait on the bank, offering a towel, and even the towel is quick and alive. From the opposite bank two apostles watch gravely. One of them, beardless, with a low forehead and deep-set eyes, turns away to look at the spectator, and may be a portrait of the mosaicist.

But it is the youthful body of Christ touched with liquid white and gold which attracts the observer. He has the long legs and the deep chest of a runner in the games. Lithe and pure, he seems to arise out of the water toward the descending dove, and there is in his posture, one hand at his side and the other blessing the waters, a suggestion of exquisite tact and understanding of the strange and terrible forces gathered round him.

So it is with all the figures on the walls. The angels gambol in the gold heavens, the waters of life flow over jeweled fountains, and the apostles walk with a grave serenity which owes as much to classical Greece as to the memory of Syria. Here the world is displayed on a field of rubies and emeralds so rich that it is almost past belief; yet the artist has made it credible. Quite suddenly, when you enter this church, there is heard the singing of angels.

Vast spaces on the walls are whitewashed plaster. More than three-quarters of the original mosaics are lost. There is no Judgment before Pilate, no Carrying of the Cross. There is only a fragment of the Temptation. And somehow it hardly matters. So much has been preserved that the imagination can easily supply the missing details. One would have thought it would be impossible to combine these pure classic forms with Christian feeling, but no: they are there. The Archangel Michael with his jeweled scepter and incandescent wings is a portrait of Apollo or the winged Dionysus; the Virgin wears the robes of Athene; Joseph beneath the olive tree harks back to Poseidon; and Christ is the young hero in the splendor of his youth.

THE FACE OF GOD

There is, on the central dome at Daphni, a mosaic so extraordinary that it seems to sum up and complete the entire course of Greek art. It goes back to the most ancient days and the most ancient beliefs, at once Christian and pagan. It says what no one else has ever dared to say.

One cannot compare this portrait of the Creator, the Pantocrator, ruler over all things in the universe, with any other mosaic, because it stands supreme among all the representations of God. No other mosaic speaks with such authority. It is not the face of power, for it goes beyond power; nor of sadness, for it goes beyond any grief; nor of majesty, for it goes beyond any imaginable kingship. Here is God in all his starkness and plainness, in his terror and beauty, in his terrifying solicitude for all created things. Here the unsayable has been said.

I know now only the beginnings of that face: it is a mosaic to be studied over many years, on many visits to Greece. No black-and-white illustration recaptures the pallor of the face set against the shimmering gold heavens, or the delicacy of the blue cruciform halo, the blue of pebbles in a mountain stream. The dark blue mantle and the gown of reddish purple have a richness and a turbulence which are not to be seen elsewhere. Those gnarled and rootlike hands, one finger of each hand separated to demonstrate the trinity, push back the walls of heaven to enable God to show himself; and the heavens crack wide open. There are strange markings and scorings on the face. There are strange words coming from the closed lips. There is a strange beauty in the desolate severity of that face. It is not a face which offers hope, for it is not concerned with anything so rash as hoping. It says what has to be said, and all its strangeness is consummated in the simplicity of the rainbow which encircles it.

We have heard of gods who spoke with the voice of thunder, but no one else ever portrayed a God who so evidently spoke out of the whirlwind. He says: "Be still, and know that I am God." But though he demands stillness, he speaks out of the tempest and there is the rage of creation in him. He is not still, nor silent, nor gentle, nor kind. He is God in all his awful majesty and power, demanding that those who have received from him the gift of life shall be obedient to his purposes.

Demanding; and being obeyed; and also being worshiped with utter abandonment in his own temple, where the walls depict the mysteries of his earthly life. Yet he is infinitely remote from those mysteries. He does not glance at them. They are the decorations of his temple only. The face suggests even more awful mysteries, which have taken place in heaven.

So he peers down over the rim of heaven with an air of godlike composure and godlike rage; not that he is unpleased with the works of man, but that he demands from them the ultimate gift of themselves. He is Christ, but he is also Jehovah, the leader of the battle hosts.

What is astonishing is that an artist with a few thousand colored stones could make a portrait of God so vivid, so comprehensive and so terrible that it gives an impression of finality.

There must have been a time when an artist sketched out the design on paper; when workmen clinging to scaffolding transferred the sketch to the dome and went on to fill out the portrait with color. Yet it is almost unthinkable that this God was ever made. It is so perfect a thing that it seems to have come into existence of its own accord.

One sees it best lying down at full length on the floor. The shimmering gold background gives it resplendent life; it is never still. The innumerable planes of the mosaic, all of them slightly tilted, have the effect of creating constant new sources of light and shadow. The face comes closer. There is nowhere where the eye can rest. A hundred glittering wedges of color form the face; hundreds more form the mantle and gown; the fingers are wedges of color, and so are the mouth and nose and the clasps of the book; even the rainbow is formed of wedges, of spikes of color. Yet we are no nearer the heart of the mystery by discovering the prevailing pattern. Although it is incontrovertibly formed of wedges that are nearly always thin and narrow, and the whole design could have been formed, not with mosaics, but with brilliantly colored splinters of glass, what is chiefly remarkable is how the artist, against all odds, succeeded in giving fluidity to those sharp angles. The glinting ax heads become flowing rivers.

Every device known to the Byzantine artists has been consciously employed to suggest the fierce solicitude of God for those who live on earth below. The eyes look away, but they also look deep into the eyes of the beholder, and this has been accomplished by the heavy curved brows and pouches which are so cunningly arranged that there seem to be two pairs of eyes, and there is even another eye, remote and mysterious, in the forehead. But the eyes that gaze impassively into the distance have not the searching power of the eyes that gaze upon the beholder. God directs his gaze everywhere, but he especially directs it upon those who offer him their most desperate and fervent prayers.

But it is the lower part of the face which expresses most succinctly the formidable power of the divine body charged with the energy of the Incarnation. The beard and mouth have the shapes of mountains, dark, craggy, beyond the power of anyone to climb them. Look at the face upside down, and you see those strange two-pinnacled mountains which appear so often on Chinese paintings. Here are the Shining Cliffs of Delphi turned dark with age. Here too are gulfs and unbridgeable chasms, roads where no mortal has ever traveled, precipices hidden in black mists. In the gaunt landscape of his face all is darkness and brooding terror except for the eyes, those quiet lakes.

This is a God who has been raised from the dead, who has been down to Hell, who has stormed Heaven. He has power to quicken, and power to kill. His gnarled and massive hands could shake the world's foundations if they wanted to; lightning comes from them. He is the God of terrible aspect, standing in judgment over the quick and the dead.

Terror lurks in that face, but it is not the terror of judgment. It is the terror of absolute divinity, of absolute justice and absolute solicitude. This is the God who cares and never ceases from caring. He is the God of the Last Day, but also of the First Day. From him come the angels with the flaming swords.

At the same time he is a purely Greek God, and he bears a remarkable resemblance to surviving images of the Olympian Zeus found on coins. Fifteen hundred years separate the ivory face of Olympian Zeus and the chalk-white face of the Christian Pantocrator, but very little has changed. There is a greater austerity, a greater clarity, a greater authority, but there is enough in common to suggest that they derive from the same mysterious sources. There is a quality of brooding, as of one contending with elemental forces and mastering them, which we see on the gold mask of Agamemnon, but Agamemnon remains among men or among the lesser gods, while the Pantocrator at Daphni is wholly God.

Invisible dark thunderclouds roll across the brilliant face. He is the God who frowns, with no trace of a smile about the lips, and yet the peace of God is clearly suggested in the gold radiance and in the quiet streams of baptism which form the three arms of the Cross.

Without the blue Cross there would be only the terror of God.

There is only one other portrait of God which can be compared with this. It stands in the apse of the Cathedral at Cefalù, not far from Palermo, and was made about A.D. 1138, some fifty years later than the mosaic at Daphni. Here God is shown as the Redeemer, a figure of exquisite majesty, authority and power, but he does not speak from the thundercloud and there is no mystery in him. He stands there in a magnificent blue cloak parted to reveal the gold tunic, and in his left hand he holds the Bible open at the page which reads: "I am the Light of the World." Framed by thick rippling hair and a brown beard, he gazes quietly and benignantly at the observer. There is no sternness; in a moment he will smile. He has grace and maturity and knows all the secrets of the universe. He stands there in imperial splendor, and though only the upper part of the body is shown in the apse it is possible to imagine the whole figure down to the feet resting near the altar, and indeed the artist has arranged the figure so that we shall imagine him standing at full length, towering over us in his physical presence. Light radiates from him; blessings pour from his upraised hand. The long face is characteristically Byzantine, but there is more than a suggestion of Norman influence, in honor of the Norman princes who conquered Sicily and built the Cathedral. Youth, elegance, majesty—all these are present. One remembers the Apollo at Delos who held out his arms in very much the same way and whose benignity was also expressed by an appearance of the utmost nobility.

The magnificence of Christ has never been portrayed with so much authority as in this figure in the apse of the Cathedral at Cefalù. There are comparable portraits in Monreale and the Cappella Palatina, but they have none of this streaming radiance, this power to evoke the heavenly majesty. Apollo at Delos proclaimed himself the God of light. The Redeemer at Cefalù proclaims himself the Light of the World. They speak to the same need in the human soul. The Pantocrator at Daphni could destroy the entire universe with his little finger if he felt that mankind was unworthy of him. He belongs to a new, a more rigorous, a more terrible dispensation.

There is perhaps no place on earth where the terror of God, the *tremendum maiestatis,* is so perfectly made manifest as in the small dome at Daphni, and nowhere is his magnificence displayed with greater power than at Cefalù.

The Pantocrator at Daphni appalls, but he also gives strength. One comes away, into the quiet courtyard, with a sense of gratitude for the image of God made plain at last. The bees are humming. The sun-baked stones quiver in the heat, and in the pine woods the birds are singing. Not far away, within a small stone's throw, the heavy trucks from Athens are roaring along the main highway to Eleusis.

The Pantocrator, Daphni

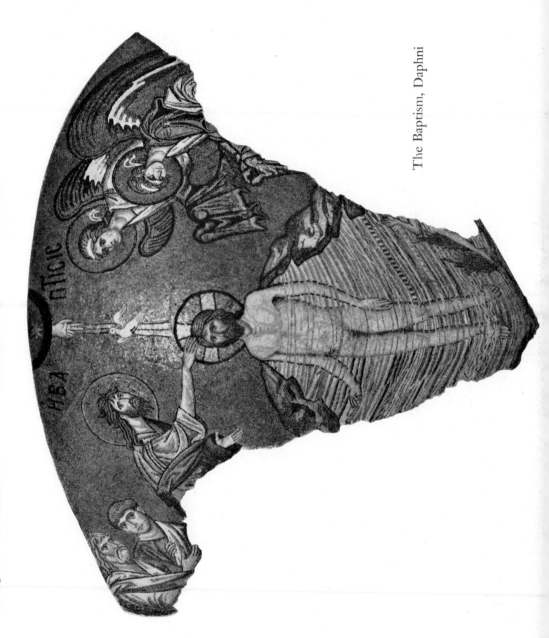

The Birth of Aphrodite on the Ludovici Throne, Museo Nazionale, Rome ◀

The Baptism, Daphni

Votive offering of Ninnion

The Aphrodite of Rhodes

Head of Woman in Ecstasy, Museo Nazionale, Rome

Botticelli. The Virgin Crowned, Uffizi, Florence

Temple of Athene at Lindos

XIII ELEUSIS

Only a few miles separate Daphni from Eleusis—the most beautiful church in Christendom from the ruined temple of the Eleusinian mysteries. Daphni lies quiet among the pines. Eleusis is a loud, bustling modern town, deafened by the explosions of gunpowder from the nearby quarries and the continual thudding of triphammers. Orange smoke belches from a score of chimneys, to drift over the Bay of Salamis. Of the great complex of buildings where the purest of all the Greek mysteries was performed, there remain only a few broken columns, some steps cut into the rock face, an eerie emptiness.

Huge walls once enclosed the sacred place; emperors and tyrants vied with one another for the honor of embellishing the gates and the temple precincts; and for generation upon generation men came to look upon the sacred wheat and to learn from the lips of the priests the secret of immortal life.

The Parthenon remains. Delphi and Olympia possess a recognizable splendor. Eleusis has been battered flat by invading armies, and the wild barley grass grows where there were marble palaces for a goddess more ancient than Apollo.

One should come in the evening to those broken fields set below a rocky cliff, with the blue bay and the purple hills of Salamis lying darkly mysterious in the sunset. Best of all to come in moonlight when the broken stones gleam like ghostly fish in the silver darkness.

There was a time when people gathered from the ends of the

earth to attend the mysteries. Millions upon millions of worshipers swore an oath of secrecy, and kept it so well that even now we cannot be certain we know exactly what took place. There was the offering of the immortal wheat, the bread of life. There was an altar, and a kind of high mass. There was a pageant in which the blessings of the afterlife were displayed. In ways still unknown the Eleusinian mysteries seem to have profoundly affected Christianity.

In the beginning there were only the footfalls of a weeping goddess who was searching for her lost daughter. She wandered helplessly along the shore, below the citadel of King Keleos which occupied the ridge. She was all women weeping for their lost children. At last she found a stone to rest on; and afterward the place where she rested was called the Laughless Stone.

No one had ever seen her before. No one knew she was the most powerful of goddesses, sister to Zeus, queen of the underworld and of all growing things. The daughters of King Keleos hurried to help her and brought her to the palace, but she refused to be helped; she refused even the offer of barley broth until the old nurse Iambe uttered an obscene oath, and then she melted a little, though she still suffered from a rage of grief. And so she remained in the palace, a foreigner, utterly disconsolate, until it occurred to King Keleos to entrust her with his sickly son. She gave the boy a bath and then raked a deep hole in the embers of the fire, and put him in. The boy's mother was hiding in the nursery and snatched her son from the flames. Demeter sprang forward to snatch the child back, but the screaming of the queen of Eleusis shocked her. "Unhappy woman, for having broken the spell," the goddess said, and suddenly she removed her hood, and her corn-colored hair fell to the ground, and she had the burning eyes of a goddess, and the look of power.

It is all the wildest of fairytales: the old crone, the broken spell, the child in the fire, the curses she rained down on the kingdom. Afterwards she took the boy in her arms and announced that henceforth he would become her servitor, distributing the corn among men.

Triptolemus came from the fire, and soon Persephone emerged from the earth, from a cave in the rocks not far from the Laughless Stone. She who had been a goddess was a goddess no longer, for she had eaten a pomegranate in her sojourn under the earth; and now she was doomed to spend four months of the year in Hades and the remaining eight months in the service of her mother. She was given a name—Korê, the Maiden. So there came into existence the first sacred family in Greece. It was a strange family, for there was no father in it, only the Mother, the Maiden and the Child.

This is all we know about the original mystery of Eleusis, which for two thousand years dominated the Greek world. In time there were to be additions to the mystery; strange elements were added to form the vast ritual of celebration; complexity was piled upon complexity. But in the very beginning—it was one of the things the Greeks never forgot—there was an old woman shaking with unappeasable grief sitting alone on the rocky shore. Eleusis means "the Coming"; and the Coming of Demeter was the coming of grief into the world.

As we see her today in the statues, sitting in majesty with the scepter of power in her hands, she wears a truly Greek appearance. Calm and composed, she gazes out at the world with a look of untroubled maturity. She is far from being the goddess of fertility; she rules over the ordered rows of corn, the careful husbandry. She has much in common with the goddess Isis, from whom perhaps she is descended; for we know from the burial pits of Eleusis that the Egyptians traded there and left behind curious objects connected with the worship of Isis dating from the XVII dynasty, about 1500 B.C. Isis, too, was a corn goddess, and like Demeter she wore the corn wreath and was attended by serpents and carried a mysterious woven basket and a winnowing fan, and went in search of her beloved. Isis searched for Osiris, her brother and husband. Demeter searched for her daughter. It is an important difference, suggesting that in the very earliest times the Greeks attributed even greater powers to the virgin goddess than to the gods; for it is Persephone who returns from the dead.

When Persephone was given back to her, Demeter ordered the Eleusinians to build a great temple on a rocky eminence below the walls of the citadel, and this too was significant. The Athenians placed their goddess Athene in the citadel, on the Acropolis, overlooking the plain; the temple of Demeter was carved against the side of a hill, hugging the earth, close to the shore. Her home was on the mysterious edge of things, where land and sea meet, and the wildfowl hover. To the end she remained a lonely goddess, almost unapproachable, hidden in her temple-cave which faced out to sea.

Over the centuries her worship was cultivated all over Greece. In late summer when the harvest was gathered in and the fields fell asleep, heralds were sent throughout Greece to proclaim the truce of the goddess and safe passage for those who wished to attend her rites. From all over Greece they came with gifts for the goddess, and ships put in at Piraeus, loaded with pilgrims from Asia Minor. According to Pausanias, there were two festivals greater than any others: they were at Olympia and Eleusis. The festivals at Delphi in honor of Apollo and at Athens in honor of Athene were important, but did not touch the hearts of people so deeply.

When Eleusis was conquered by the Athenians, Athens insisted that some part of the worship of Demeter should take place in the shadow of the Acropolis; and so there was built in Athens a special temple for the goddess called the Eleusinion, and there on the fourteenth day of the month Boedromion, at the time of the full moon, she was brought on a donkey, accompanied by her attendants. There she remained for five nights like a captive in a foreign land.

On the day after her arrival, candidates for initiation flocked to the Eleusinion to gaze on her and the sacred objects surrounding her, and to receive their catechism from the priests, and to be entered into the books. Each candidate had to be sponsored by an Athenian citizen who had himself been initiated. He must be a Greek and able to speak Greek, and those who had committed murder or other serious crimes were excluded. Otherwise, anyone who could find a sponsor could take part in the mystery. Women and slaves and beggars and those who had committed small crimes, all were free to come. So much importance was attached to the procession from Athens to Eleusis that it was placed in the hands of the *archon basileus,* one of the chief rulers of Athens.

During the days of catechism the initiates were trained in the service of the goddess. They were taught how to behave during the ceremonies; they fasted and purified themselves, and were forbidden to eat crab, gurnet or beans. "Every initiate knows why this is so," says Pausanias slyly, "and therefore I need not explain." On one of those days the initiates were assembled at a nearby gate, each one accompanied by a young pig, and the order was given: "*Mystae*, to the sea!" Then they ran down to the sea, driving their pigs before them, and then they washed themselves and the pigs in the sea. They wore their hair free, with a purple ribbon round the forehead, and a garland of myrtle, and they were dressed in long purple tunics covered with symbolic embroideries. A torchbearer and a herald, both important functionaries, accompanied them. On the seashore the initiates sacrificed the pigs and sprinkled themselves with the blood.

The young pigs, the young corn, the young god—in the Greek fashion they celebrated all that was young, while worshiping the mother of the ageless earth.

On the nineteenth day of the month they gathered at the Double Gate of Athens for the fourteen-mile journey along the Sacred Way to Eleusis. They wore their purple robes and carried long stalks of fennel, in which Prometheus had hidden the fire of Heaven, and they were crowned with myrtle. At the head of the procession went, not Demeter, but the joyful god of fertility, Iacchos, who was one of the forms of Dionysus. He was the forerunner, the herald of the feast; the Athenians were tempted to regard him as the brother of Perse-phone.

So the long procession set out, the priests marching ahead, the torchbearers in their royal robes, the crowds flocking around the statues and shouting: "Iacche! Iacche!" It was September, the hottest month of the year, and the dust rose, and the musicians played, and hymns were sung. It was a gay procession, even a rowdy one, with frequent pauses for libations, sacrifices and ceremonial dances; and much banter, and some obscenity before the shrines of the gods and heroes along the way. One of their hymns is recorded by Aristophanes in *The Frogs*:

> *O Demeter, queen of the harvest,*
> *Crowned with the ears of corn,*
> *We sing this hymn for thee,*
> *Goddess of pure mystery.*

Bless therefore thy singers,
May they walk freely
Safe from all dangers
With hilarity
And gravity
Worthy of the feast.

O Dionysus, king of song,
Thou who walkest beside the goddess,
Thou who leadest the dance,
Wanderer in ancient pathways,
Bless therefore our footsteps,
May we dance freely
Safe from all dangers
With hilarity
And gravity
Worthy of the feast.

And having announced the sacred hymns, the chorus breaks off and reproduces a fragment of conversation heard along the Sacred Way. "Just now I saw through the corner of my eye a ravishing girl, with her nipples bursting through a rent in her tunic. O Dionysus, king of the dance, guide my footsteps."

But if there was a good deal of happy obscenity on the journey, there were also many important duties to be performed, with the proper solemnity. Bursts of laughter gave place to sudden silence, and for long periods the procession halted. At the Sacred Lake, all the initiates bared their arms and legs which were bound with saffron-colored ribbons symbolizing the power of the young corn over them. So many were these pauses that it was dark before they reached Eleusis, by the light of flaming torches.

It was "the night of torches," with all the initiates running up and down the shore holding their torches aloft, so they resembled swarms of fireflies. "The meadows sparkle with a thousand fires," says the chorus in *The Frogs*. "The old shake off their years, and their limbs grow iron-strong as they dance." During that night each initiate made his way to the Laughless Stone and sat on it. No one had yet entered the precincts of the temple. That was to come later. Meanwhile the priests of Demeter uttered a last warning against the impure who might want to enter the temple—those who harbored evil thoughts, those who had committed crimes.

Men and boys raced along the shore, waving their torches wildly. Women and girls walked more sedately, with oil lamps on their heads, so that there were two patterns, two rhythms, in the furious illumination on the shore. Except for the torches and the great glow from the altar fire of the temple of Artemis-before-the-Gate, which lay outside the entrance to the temple of Demeter, there was little light, for the full moon was six days past. So they spent the night shouting and singing hymns and imitating Demeter in her search for Persephone, and in the morning they slept.

They did not sleep for long, for there were more exercises and preparations before they were permitted to enter the temple. They came crowding into the great forecourt, men and women from all over Greece, utterly silent now, each with his sponsor, all waiting for the moment when they would be allowed into the temple itself, very serious. They no longer carried their torches. Not all the men wore long purple cloaks; some wore fawn skins with the head of the spotted fawn lying against the breast. The girls wore purple tunics girded with a cord, with oriental-looking turbans wound round their heads, and they were not allowed to wear jewels or metals or cosmetics of any kind. All were barefoot, and they wore their clothes lightly, so that they could slip out of them easily. They were to approach the goddess in nakedness.

So far all the authorities are in agreement, but no one knows for certain what happened within the temple. Of "the things done, the things seen, the things shown" we have only the records of Christians who wrote at second hand. We know that the initiates were greeted by a herald who issued his last summons: "Children of men, about to pass through death, draw near," and then they whispered the password and were blindfolded and entered the sacred courts, but beyond this we know little.

To each of the initiates there was granted a vision, but we do not know the exact nature of this sudden theophany which came at the end of a long and exhausting service. Of this ultimate rite it was not permitted to speak. "A great awe of the gods holds back the voice," says the *Homeric Hymn to Demeter,* and the Greeks who were sworn to secrecy kept their oath of silence.

For an hour, for two hours they walked blindly within the many-pillared temple, deafened by the sound of rushing waters, by thunder, by music, by hymns and invocations, by all the known devices which would lead the initiate into an emotional state where he would be receptive to the final mystery. Invisible hands clutched at him; invisible pits opened before him; and he was caught before he could fall headlong. In horror and agony he was brought to the edge of madness. Whips cracked; stones fell on him; smoke choked him; snakes clung to him; and strange voices whispered to him. No one knows how long the initiate wandered in the darkness, but we know that the terror increased until it became almost unendurable, for we are told: "The nearer the goal, the greater the terror."

At last quite suddenly all the implements of terror—the whips, the snakes, the stones—gave place to the instruments of blessedness. Out of the underworld the initiate emerged into the clear world of the gods, the candles, the thrones, the brightness of the shrine where Persephone appeared in majesty, holding in her arms a sheaf of corn as one would hold a child; and she gave an ear of corn to the initiate, gave him a jug filled with water, gave him a blessing and a command: "Let the rain fall, let the seed flower." Then a whole sheaf of wheat was placed in his arms and he was led to a throne: he had become Persephone: and the priests danced round him in homage.

As a final gift the initiate received the sacred barley broth, the *kykeon,* which Demeter received from the hands of the princesses when she first arrived on the shore of Eleusis. Then having learned the watchword the initiate returned to his own home.

Only one detailed painting of the Eleusinian mysteries has survived. It is a tablet of quite remarkable complexity and beauty, offered by the young woman Ninnion as a memorial of her initiation. She has kept her oath. She does not tell all. She merely suggests in three separate registers the most important stages of the initiation. We see her at the bottom left being carried in the arms of a priest wearing a myrtle crown. The god Dionysus leads the way through the darkness, past the gleaming *omphalos,* symbol of rebirth, and the crossed myrtle branches, which are symbols of purity, into the presence of Persephone enthroned, holding her scepter in one hand and with the other offering the ear of white wheat.

On the upper register there is a blaze of light indicated by the brilliant necklaces. Now Persephone herself is leading Ninnion into the presence of Demeter, taking her by the hand. On her head Ninnion wears the sacred winnowing fan, and two priests follow her, one holding a pair of cymbals hanging from a cord, the other presenting her with a jar of barley broth. We see her for the third time in the pediment as she sits under the shadow of the winnowing fan, and one priest is again offering her the jar, and the other is clashing cymbals together. She smiles gently. The initiation is over, and she is received into blessedness. It is the moment when she sings the words which have been handed down by the Church Fathers:

> *I have eaten out of the drum,*
> *I have drunk out of the cymbals,*
> *I have carried the winnowing fan,*
> *I have entered the bridal chamber.*

Though we shall never know exactly how the mystery was conducted, we know enough to recognize that it answered a deeply felt need. There were mysteries within the mystery. The initiate confronted the god, became the god, sat in the place of splendor, and returned to his daily life with the knowledge that he had accomplished a miraculous journey which was no less miraculous because he was accompanied by thousands of others.

Nearly all Athenians were initiates. Socrates and Plato both saw the vision of immortality in the ear of wheat. Hadrian and Marcus Aurelius made special journeys to Eleusis in order to be initiated. It was a mystery for the strong, not for the weak and credulous.

"At Eleusis," said the rhetorician Aristides, "we find the common meeting-place of the earth. Of all the divine graces accorded to man, it is the most terrible, and the most marvelous. Can one name any other place where more splendid myths have been sung, or where dramas of more wonderful meaning have been performed? Generations of the blessed, both men and women, have witnessed these strange apparitions, and where else can such things be seen?"

Many others besides Aristides spoke approvingly of the mystery. They spoke of the sense of holiness which came to all those who entered the sacred precincts, and how this holiness never left them. They were touched with a divine grace. Pindar hints at the nature of the mystery when he said: "Blessed is he who, having seen all this, goes beneath the earth; he knows the end of life, and he knows its god-sent beginning."

Except a corn of wheat fall into the ground and die, it abideth alone; but if it die, it bringeth forth much fruit.

XIV   CORINTH

Nothing is lovelier than a drive along the coastal road from Eleusis to Corinth on a clear summer day. The air tumbles like a waterfall, the sea is all melting blue, and the tawny mountains with their lion flanks seem to come alive. No wonder the ancient Greeks saw gods everywhere, in mountains and seas and every bird and flower.

This, of course, is one of the troubles of traveling in Greece: the landscape seems to quiver, to be alive, to be waiting to speak. There is such a sweetness in the air, so many invisible wings beating in the high heavens, so much animal strength in the mountains that you have the impression that the whole earth is penetrated with the sap of young life, and the sky is penetrated with it, and you yourself are penetrated with it. On a summer day, traveling along that coast, no one would be surprised if Aphrodite or Poseidon rose from the waves.

But curiously, there were only the cliffs and the long stretches of empty blue sea, ghostly and mysterious, shimmering quietly, with a silver sun track wavering over it. The sea is so strangely quiet, and there are hardly any other automobiles along the road, which clings to the side of the cliffs. You expect trucks, bringing the produce of the Peloponnese to Athens, but there are none—only the clear, brilliant emptiness, the eerie silence.

Megara lies inland, white-washed walls huddled on a low hill a mile from the sea. Once there was a great wall leading from the city to the port of Nisaea, but the wall has crumbled away, Nisaea has vanished, and there are only black goats wandering among the barley grass where once there was a constant traffic of chariots. Euclid was born in Megara, and here Virgil caught the fever which led to his death.

Megara is dead, or nearly dead. Once it guarded the approach to the Peloponnese and rivaled Athens in its splendor. It had a great temple, a university, a stadium. It sent its fighting ships out to sea, and had a vast army. There was a brief period when it might have snatched from the Athenians the mastery of Greece, but there was a fatal element in the blood of its people. Thinking they held the balance of power between Corinth and Athens, they sided now with one, now with the other, and in the end were hated by both.

The highroad avoids Megara, as though to escape contamination with a dying town. There follows the wild and beautiful hugging of the cliffs, which the ancients knew as *Kaki Skala,* the Evil Stairs. Here Theseus, coming from Troezen to Athens, encountered the robber Sciron and slew him. Sciron had the unpleasant habit of making his captives wash his feet on a bare outcrop of rock overlooking the sea, and when his feet were washed, he kicked his victims over the cliffs. The sea turtles devoured them, and Sciron liked to say: "It is good to feed the turtles." When Theseus killed the robber in fair fight, he made sure that Sciron would suffer the fate he had meted out to others, but the turtle which fed on him was turned to stone. A rock, which only vaguely resembles a turtle, is pointed out as the place where Sciron met his death.

There was another side to the story, told by the people of Megara. In their eyes Sciron was a tollkeeper, who exacted only a very small toll on travelers which he contributed to the public treasury. Theseus refused to pay the toll, which accounted for the unfortunate quarrel. The people of Megara regarded it as only one more example of the barbarity of the Athenians.

Suddenly there is an end to the Evil Stairs, and the road swings inland toward the isthmus, a long plain lying at the foot of the mountains, windswept, with only pines and olive trees. Innumerable battles have been fought on the plain, but now it is only a small forgotten corner of Greece.

When you reach the isthmus, you wonder what the fuss was about. It is so small a thing that standing on a bridge over the canal you have the feeling that two or three hundred workmen equipped with bull-dozers could have dug it in a week. In fact, the French company which began digging it in 1882 never succeeded in completing it, and it was eleven years later before a Greek company completed it. Thousands of men worked their way through the soft rock, which crumbled easily, with the result that there were continual landslips. The landslips still occur. Today only the smallest ships can pass through this narrow crack which unites the Gulf of Corinth with the Saronic Gulf.

The canal is as straight as a knife blade, and the sides rise sheer from the water. Seen from the air it is an amazing spectacle, like a heavy blue line engraved relentlessly across the earth, but seen from the bridge it wears the air of an improvisation. It is odd that it should be accounted one of the great canals of the earth, to be mentioned in the same breath as Suez and Panama.

For centuries the tyrants of Greece and Rome dreamed of immortalizing themselves by cutting the canal. Periander seems to have been the first. He was followed by Demetrius Poliorcetes, Julius Caesar, Caligula and Nero. Just before his assassination, when he was preparing the invasion of Persia, Caesar sent his engineers to Corinth to plan the cutting of the canal, to make the invasion easier. Caligula, too, sent engineers to Corinth, but like Caesar he was murdered before the first spade was turned. Only Nero actively set to work and began digging.

Nero even did some digging with his own hands. At one of the most extraordinary spectacles of his spectacular reign, he presided over the inauguration of the Neronic Canal. He believed the canal would be one of the crowning achievements of his career. Everything was staged to the last detail. On the day of the ceremony he emerged from his tent, singing an ode he had composed for Amphitrite and Poseidon and all the other gods and goddesses of the sea. To the crowds who assembled from all directions he announced his joy in beginning so famous a work. The governor of Achaea presented him with a golden spade, and he dug up the first ceremonial spadeful of earth and carried it away with his spade over his shoulder. He made altogether three digs, and at one of them, perhaps the last—for the records are not clear—he received a shock which momentarily paralyzed him: where he was digging, the earth exuded a heavy red liquid like blood.

Nero was an unusually superstitious man, and he may have remembered that the sage Apollonius of Tyana had pronounced a mysterious prophecy seven years before. Apollonius had said: "This neck of land shall be cut through, or rather it shall not." It was believed that a curse hung over any attempt to dig the canal, a belief which was encouraged by the Corinthians who earned a living by hauling ships on rollers over the isthmus. Nero seems to have remained for some days at Corinth, watching his workmen digging through the rock. Among them were 6,000 Jews sent by Vespasian from Jerusalem.

A few months later Nero was stabbed to death by his own secretary, and the digging of the canal came to an abrupt end. Then for more than nineteen hundred years no attempt was made to carve through that soft and treacherous earth. The haulers were happy. Along greased sleds they pulled and dragged the ships from the Bay of Corinth over a low hill covered with gorse and scrub and windblown pine trees, and let them down on the other side. They had fought against the making of the canal from the beginning, and for some two thousand five hundred years they remained in business.

THE TEMPLE OF APOLLO

When the Greeks woke up in the morning they would go to their doors, gaze up at the sun and blow a kiss to Apollo.

I used to think this was the most charming gesture imaginable. I am not so sure now. I suspect they threw a kiss to Apollo out of their love for him, but also because they were a little afraid of him, as children will run and kiss someone who needs to be placated. They knew, as we know, that Apollo was the lord of music and song, but he was also the bringer of sudden death. In Greece the sun kills.

There is a story of a German archaeologist who proclaimed loudly at Delphi that Apollo was not a sun god at all, but a very minor deity of no particular importance. He took the long goat path which winds not far from the Phaedriades to the bleak and empty plains at the top of Parnassus, and was found there some days later. He had died of sunstroke.

I remembered the German archaeologist as I wandered across the rubble-strewn field which is all that remains of ancient Corinth. The sun blazed in a violet sky. The gleaming shoulder of Acrocorinth, the great hill which rises gently above the abandoned city, acted like a burning glass, throwing the sun's golden rays down on the rolling plain. The heat struck off every stone, and even the lizards moved slowly in the shadow of the dry grasses. There was no shade except for the small shadow thrown by the columns of the temple of Apollo —seven thick squat columns, very powerful, but with no particular beauty of grace. Standing under the columns, you could feel the heat welling out of the ancient stone.

Corinth suffered the same fate as Aegina: it was destroyed completely and its people were thrown into slavery. Proud, it suffered the fate of the proud. There is no city now, and not much more rubble than you will find in a field in Scotland.

There was a time when Corinth was the richest port in the eastern Mediterranean, when thousands of houses and villas stood along the shore and climbed halfway up the slopes, and when every sailor who entered the harbor paid tribute to the "armed Aphrodite" whose shrine stood on the summit of Acrocorinth. It was the most populous city of ancient Greece, with the greatest wealth, the greatest number of warehouses, the largest banks and the most prostitutes. All the arts of luxury were cultivated, and the most beautiful courtesans paraded through the streets. Corinth was the founding mother of colonies in Syracuse and Corcyra, and her coins, stamped with the winged horse, were second only to the coins of Aegina in value. A million people once lived where now there is no one at all. The long thistle grass; stones tumbled on stones; the seven pillars of Apollo; an ancient well; nothing else.

One wonders how it could ever have been allowed to fall into decay, for it is impossible to imagine a more beautiful site. The earth cries out for a city to be built here, on the slope between the blazing yellow shield of Acrocorinth and the somnolent set, a blue haze of mountains across the gulf. The air is invigorating. The heat strikes hard, but it is a tolerable heat. One imagines a city like Algiers, terrace upon terrace facing the sea, palm trees, temples, shady walks under marble porticos. Almost you can reconstruct the city in the imagination. You open your eyes wide, and there is only a crumbling stone platform, and the lizards crawling.

Corinth is not a ruin like Olympia. It is a desert.

The temple of Apollo dominates the desert. Those reddish columns have more power and energy in them than any columns I have seen in Greece or Sicily. They can never have been beautiful; they are heavy and deliberate; they speak of a god's self-assurance and his determination to survive. There must have been at least twenty temples in Corinth at the height of its power, but only these seven columns survive.

There is an oasis in the desert, but it cannot be seen from the plain. A stone's throw from the temple lie the charming underground grottoes known as the springs of Peirene, named after a nymph who dissolved into tears when Artemis accidentally killed her son.

Once these grottoes were on the same level as the city, but the detritus of centuries covered them. The archaeologists searched for them in vain until it suddenly occurred to them that they would have to dig deep to find them. They are reached by steps leading into an enclosed garden, where there are banana trees and everything is in flower. The tears of Peirene can be heard falling. They make a very sweet musical sound as they flow past ornamental gates painted with leaping fish and tumbling dolphins. The paint is flaking away; the fish and dolphins will not last much longer. It was pleasant to stay there among the green shadows, far from the scorching plain.

Perhaps it was the destiny of Corinth to be utterly destroyed. Inevitably the city grew rich from its commanding position; inevitably it gave way to luxury and thought itself impregnable; and just as inevitably it incurred the envy of Athens and Rome. It seems to have been under a curse from the beginning.

The Corinthians themselves relished the stories of the ancient heroes who lived under a curse.

What monsters they were! There was Sisyphus, who founded the city and who was so hated and despised by the gods that he was punished by being made to push a huge boulder uphill, but whenever he came near the crest the boulder hurtled to the bottom and he had to begin again. His crime was overweening pride, and his whole family suffered from the same sin. His son Glaucus was torn to pieces by his own mares because he laughed at Aphrodite. His grandson Bellerophon was even more impious: on his winged horse Pegasus he set out to slay the fire-breathing Chimaera, and having slain it, he believed himself powerful enough to invade the haunts of the gods on Mount Olympus: his punishment was to wander like a ghost forever in the Luckless Fields. From Bellerophon's grandson, who fought beside Hector in the Trojan War, came the saddest of Greek cries of doom:

> *Men in their generations are like the leaves*
> *Which the winds scatter over the earth:*
> *The fresh buds burst forth in the spring.*
> *So it is with mortals: one flourishes, another ceases.*

Doom touched nearly all the heroes who came to Corinth. After he had led the Argonauts to Colchis, Jason came to Corinth with Medea, and lived happily until he fell in love with Glauce, the king's daughter. Medea sent Glauce a poisoned robe, and she died in agony. Medea was not content with killing her rival, but went on to kill Jason's children as well. Jason spent his last years wandering in solitude beside the Saronic gulf until one day when he was lying under his beached ship the poop of the *Argo* fell on him and crushed him to death.

This is only the beginning of the long catalogue of horrors connected with the rulers of Corinth. An endless procession of tyrants ruled over the city, none of them more remarkable than Periander, who for some mysterious reason came to be known as one of "the seven sages of Greece."

According to Herodotus, Periander sent a messenger to Thrasybulus, the tyrant of Miletus, to discover the art of government. Thrasybulus took the messenger into a field of corn and then set about lopping off all the tallest ears. "This," he said, "is the art of government." The perplexed messenger returned to Corinth, and described what he had seen, saying it was impossible to make any sense of the words of the tyrant who amused himself by an exhibition of wanton destruction. Periander knew better. He realized at once that Thrasybulus was recommending the murder of all the outstanding citizens, and he accordingly set about imitating the tyrant of Miletus.

Periander, according to Herodotus, was three-quarters mad, a pervert and a conjuror of ghosts. He had lain with his wife Melissa after he murdered her. Some time later, having lost something valuable and wanting to know where it was, it occurred to him to summon up her ghost. She complained of being cold and naked in her grave, and refused to tell him where the valuable property was hidden until he made her warm again by burning clothes in her honor. Periander thereupon ordered all the young girls and women in Corinth to appear at the temple of Hera. They thought they were coming to a festival and put on their best clothes. Armed guards surrounded the temple. All the women were ordered to strip naked, "nor," says Herodotus, "did he make any distinction between virgins and matrons." A great pit was dug, the clothes were thrown in, and then set on fire. Melissa was pleased. She was now warm in her grave, and she told him where his valuable property was hidden.

One of the pleasanter stories about Periander concerns the poet Arion of Methymna, who was credited with the invention of lyric verse. He had left the court of the tyrant and wandered through Italy and Sicily, singing his songs. When he had earned a great deal of money, he decided to return to Corinth and took a ship from Tarentum. The sailors hatched a plot to steal his money and throw him overboard. When Arion begged them to take the money and spare his life, the sailors offered to let him kill himself, and promised him a proper burial when they reached the shore. Herodotus tells the story brilliantly:

> Arion begged them to let him stand on the quarter-deck in his singing robes, while he gave them a song, promising that when the song was over he would kill himself. To the sailors it seemed a pleasant thing to hear the best of living singers, and so they made their way forward from the stern and assembled amidships. Then Arion wrapped himself in his robes, took up his lute and sang them a lively tune. Afterwards he leapt into the sea, still in his robes.
>
> Meanwhile the sailors continued their voyage to Corinth, but they say a dolphin carried Arion on its back to Taenarum, and thence, still wearing his robes, he made his way to Corinth, where he was able to tell everything that had happened to him.

According to Herodotus, Periander was inclined to disbelieve the story until the sailors arrived in Corinth. He asked them what had happened to Arion, and they answered that they had left him safely behind at Tarentum. Suddenly Arion popped out of his hiding place, and confronted them. "It was," says Herodotus, "a rude shock for the sailors."

Periander's successor was assassinated after a short reign; the tyranny was succeeded by an aristocracy of merchant princes. Over many years Corinth wallowed in the dullness of habitual prosperity, taking little part in the war against the Persians, though she sent a few ships to Salamis. Corinthian luxury became proverbial; and Pindar, who reveled in luxury, celebrated in 464 B.C. the double victory of the Corinthian youth Xenophon, who won both the running race and the pentathlon at the Isthmian games, by writing a hymn in praise of a city where only virtue reigned:

> *For here dwelleth Order and Justice, the sure*
> *Foundation of cities, and Peace also, their kinswoman,*
> *Who dispenses all wealth to mankind.*

For you, Corinthians, often have the Hours
Bestowed the splendid crowns on athletes
Victorious at the sacred games, and often
You have discovered deep in your manly hearts
The ancient attributes of wisdom.
Whoever hath devised, to him belongs the deed.

It is perhaps the strangest of Pindar's hymns, for he is so determined to celebrate the Corinthians that he finds excuses for Sisyphus and Medea, and attributes wisdom to Bellerophon. Significantly his favorite cities were Corinth, Aegina and Syracuse, all of them enemies of Athens.

Corinth rejoiced in the downfall of Athens and opened her arms to Alexander the Great, who here proclaimed himself leader of the Greeks against the Persians. It was during this visit that Alexander encountered the cynic Diogenes in the garden suburb of Craneum, famous for its cypress groves. Diogenes was lying there in the sun when Alexander, accompanied by his retinue, came up to him. The philosopher raised himself a little and permitted himself a brief glimpse at the conqueror. Courteously Alexander asked if he was in need of anything. "Yes," replied Diogenes. "I would be glad if you would not stand between me and the sun." Alexander was taken aback, but when the members of his retinue burst out laughing over the strange bitterness of the philosopher, Alexander is supposed to have said: "If I were not Alexander, I would be Diogenes."

The story is too well authenticated to be dismissed. Diogenes was speaking in character, and so was Alexander. On another occasion, when Philip of Macedon was advancing on Corinth, Diogenes laughed openly at the Corinthians who were busily putting the city in a state of defense. He girded up his blanket, and with a great show of energy went bowling a large jar up and down the Craneum. When someone asked him why he did this, he answered: "I am rolling my jar so as not to be the only idle one among so many workers." And when Dionysius of Syracuse was captured by the Corinthians and brought to live in honorable captivity in Corinth, Diogenes saluted him with the remark that he was sorry for the former tyrant. Dionysius was pleased. "Yes, I am sorry you are not still a tyrant," Diogenes went on, "for tyranny is absolute slavery, and you should have been permitted to die in the absolute slavery which is reserved for tyrants. It makes me angry to see you wandering about our streets like any free-born Corinthian." And saying that, Diogenes wandered away to his jar.

Dionysius was one of the stranger inhabitants of Corinth. Captured by the Corinthian general Timoleon and in spite of his crimes allowed to go unpunished, he spent his time pretending to be a half-wit. He liked to loiter in the fish markets or sit in the perfumer's shop or squabble with common women in the streets, and he was especially fond of debating with chorus girls about their singing. He had bled Sicily white. He was another Caligula or Nero, vicious and obscene. For some reason it amused him to invite the philosopher Plato to his court, and one day in Corinth, when Plato was dead and Dionysius was enjoying his exile, someone asked him whether the society of philosophers had given him wisdom. "Truly it is my good fortune to have known them," he replied, "for through them I have acquired the wisdom to bear my present fate." It was the custom in his court for people entering his presence to shake out the folds of their gowns to show they had no concealed weapons, and when a visitor in Corinth pointedly did the same, Dionysius observed quietly: "It would be kinder if you shook your gown when leaving, then I would be sure you are not stealing anything."

Timoleon, the conqueror of Dionysius, was one of the few Corinthians who are remembered with pleasure. He was a tall, gentle soldier, ruddy-faced, with a horror of war. In one of his early campaigns he threw himself into the front lines to rescue his brother. Covering his brother Timophanes with a shield, he parried all the attacks of the enemy, and was wounded. He succeeded in saving his brother's life at great risk. Some years later his brother made himself tyrant of Corinth. Timoleon had sworn so many oaths against tyranny that he knew exactly what he had to do. He begged his brother repeatedly to divest himself of his tyrannical powers. One day he came with two others to Timophanes and for the last time begged him to divest himself of his powers. In answer Timophanes burst out laughing. Timoleon gave the sign and turned his face away, while his accomplices stabbed the brother to death.

In a long life that was the only crime he ever committed. Corinth had founded Syracuse. The gentle unassuming general was horrified by the tyranny of Dionysius. Like the Athenians before him he prepared a fleet and sailed to Sicily to put down tyranny. He went to Delphi to consult the oracle. He was on his way to the chamber where the priestess of Apollo sat on her throne when a crown which had been hanging on the wall fell onto his head; and with this blessing of the god, he landed in Sicily, fought a brief campaign and sent the tyrant into exile. When he died the people of Syracuse set his tomb in the marketplace and established annual prizes for music and horse races in his honor. "He destroyed the tyrants, overcame the barbarians, replenished the empty cities, and restored to the Greeks of Sicily the privilege of living by their own laws." Few other Greeks accomplished so much as this general with the sweet-sounding name.

Corinth celebrated its own games, where the crowns of victory were woven out of parsley. These games occurred every two years. From all over Greece men came to compete in the Isthmian games. Socrates attended them on the only known occasion when he left Athens in a time of peace. Pindar sang odes in honor of the victors. On one celebrated occasion the conqueror of Philip of Macedon, Titus Quinctius Flaminius, interrupted the games and proclaimed the full liberty of Hellas and promised that henceforth there would be no taxes or impositions of any kind. The people shouted so loud with joy that a flock of crows flying overheard shivered, as though a thunderstorm was passing. Some of the crows fell dead.

The Greeks might have known better than to trust the Roman promises. Fifty years later, in 146 B.C., Lucius Mummius won for himself the surname Achaiachus for his conquest of Greece and the establishment of the Roman province of Achaia. He defeated the army of the Greeks at the isthmus, and since the Corinthians had fought more furiously for their promised freedom than the rest, he decided to punish them by razing the city to the ground. He sold the people into slavery and ordered all the statues which had once decorated the streets and temples of Corinth to be shipped to Rome. To the ships' captains conveying this treasure to Rome he gave the famous instructions: "If any statue is destroyed, it must be replaced by another of equal value."

There is a strange story told of a young Corinthian captive who was brought into the presence of the conquering general. It amused Mummius to discover whether the boy was well educated. He told him to write something in the sand, and the boy traced in Greek the lines of Homer:

> *Thrice and four times blessed are those who fell*
> *On the plain of Troy, obeying the will of the gods.*

Mummius was deeply moved, and gave the boy his liberty. It is possible that the boy would have preferred death.

There was no Corinth: only the burning ruins and the fallen statues. Then as now the lizards crept among the tumbled stones.

XV   PATMOS

"I John, who also am your brother, and companion in tribulation, and in the kingdom and patience of Jesus Christ, was in the isle that is called Patmos, for the word of God, and for the testimony of Jesus Christ. I was in the Spirit on the Lord's day, and heard behind me a great voice, as of a trumpet, saying, I am Alpha and Omega, the first and the last: and, What thou seest, write in a book, and send it unto the seven churches which are in Asia."

So somewhere toward the end of the first century, in a cave in Patmos, wrote an old man who may have been the Beloved Disciple, in a mood of extraordinary excitement which still makes our hearts beat faster. We know when he came to the island, for St. Irenaeus tells us that it was "almost in our own generation, at the end of the reign of Domitian." Clement of Alexandria adds that John returned to his home in Ephesus "on the death of the Emperor," which occurred on September 18, A.D. 96. We know that John stayed on the island only for a little while, perhaps only for a few months, and that he preached the Gospel there, and never returned. We shall never know why he chose that barren and rocky place, but we can guess that it offered advantage to a man fleeing from persecution; for it was a place to hide in.

There are no other islands quite like this off the coast of Asia. Patmos seems to ache in its misery. It is so gaunt and sinister, so dark with beetling cliffs, so chaotic in its shapelessness. If it has any shape at all, it is that of a squashed animal in which there remains only a little flicker of life. Shadowless, treeless, scorched by the sun, it seems to be throwing out despairing cries toward Asia, which hovers faintly in the distance.

No one would live in Patmos if he could avoid it. The Greeks have almost abandoned it, leaving behind only a small scattering of peasants who live on remittances from the mainland or from the United States; and the rare tourists provide no wealth. It was the same in ancient times. The Greeks paid almost no attention to the island; it is mentioned only once in antiquity. The Romans sent their political exiles here, and the Ottoman Turks saw no advantages in possessing it and made no effort to add it to their Mediterranean empire. Pirates sailed into the narrow and treacherous bays, and there are stories of buried treasure in the caves, but no record that any has been found.

Yet there is treasure enough and to spare on the island; not in gold, though there is much gold. The treasure lies in the bleak, angry cave halfway up a hillside. The cave has been carved out of purple porphyry rock, blackened by age and smoke, and no one who ever goes there can doubt that this is the Cave of the Apocalypse. Unlike many of the sacred places on the earth, it still speaks with an authentic holiness. One can imagine John writing the *Revelation* there; it is, once you have been there, impossible to imagine him writing it anywhere else.

The roof of the cave has the shape of a wave; and indeed the whole cave seems to have been formed when a wave forced its way into the mountainside and exploded there. Inside, you are aware of the heavy dark rock flowing all round you; you become the wave; you become the rock. The golden lamps gleam and the silver altars reflect the light of the lamps, but it is not difficult to imagine the place when there was only the bare rock. The floor has been lowered; it was once much smaller, perhaps only high enough for a man to stand upright in. You can walk across it in ten paces. There is only the crowding rock, the sense of menace, darkness enfolding everything.

The black-robed priest points to the hollow where John laid his head, the little cup-shaped hole he gripped when he rose from his bed, and the shelf of rock which formed the desk of the acolyte who took down the words pouring from his lips. Above, there is the strange curving break in the rock, where the lightning struck: so the priest tells you, recounting every incident of the event as though he had been present. He does not explain why John should rest his head against a hollow now eighteen inches above the level of the floor, or why the lightning of God produced such a small scar on the rock face. In just such a cave a man might easily surrender to visions, especially on the nights of winter storms, when the whole island quaked and the lightning played on the mouth of the cave.

From the mouth of the cave John could look out on a rocky headland, a raging sea and one of the great blue cliffs of the sheltering bay. "And I saw another mighty angel come down from heaven, clothed with a cloud: and a rainbow was upon his head, and his face was as it were the sun, and his feet as pillars of fire: and he cried with a loud voice, as when a lion roareth." So one peal of thunder followed another, and the lightning spilled across the sea, where dragons rose and white horses plunged to their deaths and the waves gave up their dead. To anyone who knows storms in the Aegean there was nothing strange in such visions: they are the very substance of what is seen. Reading *Revelation* afresh after visiting the island, you become aware how accurately John has recorded the drama of the storm of God in terms of an earthly storm veering from one side of the rocky headland to another, the voices of the angels coming now from one direction, now from another, and always reverberating against the cliffs. How admirably he conveys the rage of the storm! How accurately he suggests man's helplessness before the ferocious lightning, the waves roaring up the cliffs, the murderous thunder echoing across the mountains. There is confusion in his recital of the event, but it is the confusion inevitable in a storm. There are many pauses, many resurrections, moments of terrible tension when the storm seems to be over but the threat of it hangs overhead; and then the storm returns more relentlessly than ever.

In the last chapter of *Revelation* John describes the City of God glittering with thousands of polished stones, gleaming like glass and shining like gold. Is this perhaps a vision based upon the island in the dawn light, when the storm is over and thousands of flooded springs and rivulets pour down the mountainside, glistening on the red and purple porphyry? At such moments the island seems to glow with an interior light. After describing the city with its gates of pearl and foundations of jasper, emerald, beryl, sardonyx, sapphire, and all the precious stones he can remember, John says: "The city had no need of the sun, neither of the moon, to shine in it: for the glory of God did lighten it, and the Lamb is the light thereof."

THE FORTRESS

You come out of the dark cave, blinking in the sunlight, past the beggars and the postcard sellers and the inscriptions announcing that this is the Cave of the Apocalypse—as though one needed any reminding—past the black-robed priests and the scrawny chickens and the cluttered vineyards, and there is no help for it but you must climb the steep mountain path to the fortress-monastery which crowns the summit like a huge bedraggled swan, moulting and tossing her feathers all over the landscape.

There is nothing in this monastery which suggests compassion or mercy; there is no quietness about it, as there is about Daphni and Hosios Lukas. It dominates the whole island with its formidable array of towers, cupolas, belfries and battlements with their connecting walks. It has the look of a Norman fortress meant to guard all the approaches of the island. When John came to the island, the mountaintop was crowned with a small temple to Artemis, goddess of the night. The temple has gone; the fortress has taken its place, and there is still something obscurely menacing about those grey walls, though they glisten white in the sun.

There seems to have been no monastery at all until the time of the Crusades, when the Byzantine Emperor Alexius I gave the island in 1088 to the saintly Christodoulos, whose embalmed body lies beside the altar: those who want to may kiss the top of his head through a silver grille. Though the monastery is enormous, stretching across acres of barren mountaintop, the church is small and cluttered, with barely room to move around in. There are frescoes on the walls, the figures of the saints dripping gold, but the gold is flaking away. There is a gilt cross given by Catherine the Great, and many Russian icons, for the Russians were always attracted to the island and sent countless presents of jewels to the monastery. Beside the door there is a grandfather clock with a painting of Amsterdam on the clock face. The ships in the foreground would move if the clock was ever wound up.

Outside the church, in the whitewashed courtyard, black-robed theological students wander. They look young, very much at their ease, with thin pointed smiles; they come from the mainland of Greece, from Syria, Lebanon and Abyssinia. In the past, hundreds of these students came from Russia, but the days of Russian domination in the island are over.

One of these students, a boy with a thin golden beard and the manners of a youthful patriarch, took us to the library and the treasury. There were the usual ecclesiastical offerings of emperors and empresses, jewel-studded crosses and miters, the frayed robes of gold cloth worn by long-dead bishops. Two pages of the famous *Codex Porphyrius* of the Gospels, written on purple parchment in gold and silver letters, could be seen under a glass case. The pages are small, not much larger than the pages of an ordinary book. Once the vellum was stained to a vivid reddish-purple, but it has now faded into blue-grey; and the silver uncials no longer glow on the page.

The *Codex Porphyrius* has been raided by collectors during the last two hundred years, so that only a fragment amounting to thirty-three leaves of the Gospel of St. Mark remains in the possession of the monastery. The monastery officials are not too dismayed: they claim to possess three original paintings by St. Luke, and not even the Vatican can make a similar claim.

The raiders came from half the countries of Europe. Edward Daniel Clarke, a famous receiver of stolen manuscripts, sold some pages to the Bodleian Library at Oxford. Six leaves were acquired by the Vatican, two are in Vienna, four are in the British Museum. The most demanding raiders were the Russians, who carried 182 leaves to St. Petersburg and presented them to the Czar.

These thirty-three leaves are nearly all that remains of the once-great library at Patmos. A white-bearded monk sighed when I asked him about the nine hundred manuscripts which are supposed to be still in the possession of the monastery. "There are only a few—only a very few," he said.

From the narrow Gothic windows of the monastery you can see the islands of Samos and Icaria floating in the violet-blue sea. The view from the windows of the treasury is especially pleasing. It was very quiet on the heights. No wind stirred in the palm trees growing nearby, and the monks as usual walked in unhurried silence.

FRIEDRICH HÖLDERLIN

The star-struck poet with the resounding name never came to Patmos during his life, but I suspect that he haunts the island in death. He hated Germany, and in imagination spent his years in Greece, "the fountain of my existence, where the waters are purest." He reveled in Pindar and Sophocles, and when he was a young student he competed with the philosopher Hegel in producing poems about the Greek gods and temples which neither of them ever saw. At the age of thirty he was struck down by a strange madness and retired from the world of the living. Like a ghost, still dreaming of Greece, he lived to be seventy-three.

The greatest of his poems is "Patmos," which he wrote in 1803. It is a strange and difficult poem, written on the model of the Pindaric odes, where the connecting links are sometimes omitted, but the reader is nearly always carried over the gaps by the passion of his imagery and the glorious violence of the verse. Generations of German students have whispered the opening lines in time of danger:

> *Nah ist*
> *Und schwer zu fassen der Gott.*
> *Wo aber Gefahr ist, wächst*
> *Das Rettende auch.*

Near is the God
And He is hard to hold.
But where there is danger
There rises the Saviour.
In the darkness dwell the eagles,
And fearless go
The Sons of the Alps over the Abyss
On lightly-built bridges.
Therefore since all round are piled
The summits of Time,
And the most-beloved dwell near, languishing on
Inaccessible cliffs,
Give us innocent water, O wings give us
That with most faithful understanding
We may go hither and return again.

So I spoke, when I was led away
By the spirit from my own home
More swiftly than I could tell,
And far, whither I never
Thought I would come. It darkened
In twilight, as I went past
The shadowy forest
And the yearning streams
Of my Fatherland. I knew these places no more;
When suddenly in new splendour
Mysteriously
Gleaming in golden haze,
Swiftly awakened
By the footsteps of the sun,
Fragrant with a thousand peaks,

Asia appeared to me, and blinded I looked
For something I knew, for the broad highways
Seemed strange to me, where down
From Mount Tmolus falls the river
Pactolus adorned with gold
And Taurus stands, and Messogis,
And full of flowers the garden,
A still fire. But in the light
There gleams high up the silver snow,

And the ancient ivy grows,
Sign of eternal life,
On inaccessible cliffs,
And the solemn,
The divinely-built palaces
Are borne on the living pillars
Of cedars and laurel.

Around Asia's portals murmuring
Stretching hither and thither
In the uncertain plain of the sea
Are shadowless roads enough,
Yet the seaman knows the islands.
But when I heard
That one of those lying near
Was Patmos,
I desired greatly
There to alight and enter
The dark grotto,
For not Cyprus rich in springs
Nor any other island
Dwells in the splendour of Patmos . . .

Once she nursed the beloved of God,
The visionary who in his blessed youth
Walked with God's son, inseparable,
And the bearer of thunder
Loved the simple soul of the disciple,
And the attentive man
Saw perfectly the face of God
When among the mysteries of the Vine
They sat together at the hour of the banquet,
And the Lord pronounced Death and the last Love,
Calmly foreknowing in his great soul,
For never had He words enough
To speak of blessedness at that time
Nor to comfort them when he saw
The world's rage. Thereupon He died. Much might
Be said of these things. To the very end
The Companions beheld his triumphant gaze,
Most joyful of all.

Yet they mourned and were amazed,
For now evening was come,
And great decisions
Had entered their souls. But they loved life
Under the sun and had no desire to depart
From the face of the Lord
And from their own homes. This was driven in them
Like fire in iron, and the shadow of the Beloved
Walked by their sides.
Therefore He sent them the Spirit
And truly the house shook
And the thunder of God rolled
Rumbling far
Over their boding heads, as deep in thought
These heroes of death were assembled.

Now when he was about to depart,
Once more He appeared to them:
But presently the Light of the Sun,
The Kingly One, was extinguished,
The straight radiance of the sceptre shattered
In divine anguish.
Yet in His appointed time
He will return. Later
It would not have been good
To break off abruptly and unfaithfully
The work of men. From now on it was joy
To live in loving night, preserving
In simple and steadfast eyes
Abysses of wisdom. And the living images
Grew green in the depths of the mountains.

But terrible it is how here and there
God endlessly scatters living things.
Hard it is to abandon
The faces of dear friends
And go alone above the mountains
Where the divine spirit, twice revealed,
Speaks nevertheless in a single voice:
There were no prophecies, but presently
The hair was seized, and suddenly
God sped into the distance

And gazed back at them, and they cried:
'Remain', naming the evil
Which was bound for ever in golden chains.
So they grasped one anothers' hands.

But when He then died,
He on whom beauty chiefly clung,
So that a miracle was wrought in His image
And the Heavenly Ones pointed to Him,
And when an eternal enigma to one another,
They who once lived in memory together
No longer comprehend one another:
And when the sand and the meadows fall away,
And the temples are toppling,
And the honor of the demi-god
And all his followers has departed,
Thereupon even the Highest
Turns away His face,
So that nowhere again
Is anything immortal to be seen in the heavens
Or on the green earth, what is this?

It is the throw of the sower when he scoops
The wheat in his shovel
And throws it into the clear, flinging it over the threshing-floor.
The chaff falls at his feet,
But in the end comes the grain.
And there is no evil if
Some of the speech is lost.
The living voice fades away,
But the divine work resembles our own.
Not all things at once does the Lord desire.
Yet the pit-shaft bears iron
And Etna its glowing resin,
So would I have wealth
To form a pure image
And see Christ as He was,

But if someone impatiently
With sorrowful speech fell upon me during a journey,
When I was defenceless,
So that I marveled and desired

To assume the image of God, myself a slave—
In wrath visibly once I saw
The Lord of Heaven, not that I should be something,
But to learn. Good they are, but most hateful to them
As long as they reign, is falsehood: for it means
That our common humanity no longer counts among men.
For they do not rule, but immortal destiny
Rules, and their work
Moves of itself, and speedily comes to an end.
Therefore when the Heavenly Triumph
Mounts higher, then the exultant
Son of God
Is named like the sun by the strong,

A watchword and here is the staff
Of Song beckoning down.
For nothing is ever debased. This song awakens
The dead who are not yet trapped into meanness.
Therefore there are many
Timid eyes waiting to see the light,
Having no desire to flower
In the penetrating beams of light,
Although a golden bridle holds their courage up.
But when,
Forgotten by the swelling brows
Of the world,
A softly gleaming power falls from Holy Scripture,
May there be joy in grace
As they peer into His silent Face.

And if the Heavenly Ones now, as I believe
Love me, how much more Thee?
For one thing I know—
The will
Of the Heavenly Father
Is wholly concerned with Thee.
Calm is His sign
In the thundering Heavens. And One stands beneath
His whole life long. For Christ lives still,
And they, the Heroes, His Sons,
And Holy Scripture—all have come
From Him. And the deeds of the world declare

The lightning till now,
An eternal race. For He is near. And all
His works are known to Him for everlasting . . .

There was nothing for it but to read the poem aloud, standing on one of the stone courses dividing the barren fields, to be nearer to the sky. I had scarcely finished when a ten-year-old girl, with blue eyes and bright yellow hair, wearing a patched red dress, appeared from nowhere with an armful of flowers.

There are a surprising number of fair-haired and blue-eyed children on the island. She asked what I was doing, and I told her as well as I could. She gave me the flowers, and then we went hand in hand to the waiting ship.

XVI   R H O D E S

Pindar tells the story of how the gods drew lots to divide up the earth, while Apollo was driving his chariot across the heavens. When Apollo learned what happened, he stormed into the assembly of the gods and demanded that the earth should be divided up again, but at that moment he espied an island lurking at the bottom of the sea. He was so astonished by the beauty of the island that he offered to let the gods keep their possessions as long as this island was given to him. They willingly gave it to him, and he called it after his sacred flower, the rose. In his honor the Rhodians sacrificed white lambs, white rams, white horses and red honey. Here he instituted games: the prize was a crown of white poplar.

Delos was the sacred island of Apollo, Rhodes his playground. The Romans spoke of "Rhodian luxury," and it is still luxurious.

Today Rhodes lies off the beaten track, but in ancient times it lay at the crossroads of empire, commanding the approaches to Egypt, Crete and Asia Minor. To survive, the Rhodians had to build a powerful fleet, and their sailors were accounted the best in the Mediterranean. Rhodes sent colonies to Sicily, Italy and France: Agrigentum, Naples and Arles (once known as Rhodanoussia) were founded by Rhodians. They took part in the Trojan war and were present at the battle of Salamis as allies of the Persians. They were traders, bankers and lawyers, and the maritime code of the Rhodians was so complete that Augustus Caesar, who had a special fondness for the island, incorporated it unchanged into Roman law.

Wealth poured into the island, so much wealth that it was always in danger of attack. When Alexander the Great died, and his successors fought for the broken pieces of his empire, the Rhodians proclaimed their independence. Demetrius Poliorcetes, "the besieger," attacked the city of Rhodes with his whole fleet, landed battering rams, catapults and siege towers, and hammered at the ramparts. There was a twelve-month siege. The defenders were so desperate that they armed the slaves and promised them their freedom if Demetrius was defeated. Demetrius brought up more siege engines, including the terrifying helepole, a huge wooden tower mounted on wheels and a hundred and thirty feet high, from which he could look over the walls and fire flaming arrows into the city at his leisure. The defenders succeeded in toppling the helepole by driving it into an artificial swamp, but the siege continued, coming to an end only when King Ptolemy of Egypt, who maintained a loose alliance with the Rhodians, sent a fleet to their rescue.

Demetrius was one of those huge, ruddy-faced men who enjoy war for its own sake, and there was no malice in him. He sailed away after paying tribute to the defenders and presenting them with his entire stock of siege engines as a gift. The Rhodians believed that Apollo had come to their rescue, and from the proceeds of the sale of the captured equipment they built a gigantic bronze statue of the god. The old Dorian word for a statue was *colossos;* the statue came to be known as the Colossus of Rhodes.

No one knows where the statue stood, whether on the mole or on the hill overlooking the harbor where the Castello now stands. But we know that it was about a hundred and twenty feet high, sixty feet around the chest, and a single thigh was eleven feet thick. Naked and lean, standing in the familiar posture of Apollo with his arms stretched before him, he gazed across the sea, and it was said that men in the crow's-nests could see him from sixty miles away. He wore a spiked crown of gold, and at night his whole figure was illuminated by flares.

The Colossus of Rhodes was the work of the sculptor Chares of Lindos. He built it of enormous plates of bronze held together internally by massive iron braces, reinforced by blocks of stone. It took him twelve years to build, but within fifty years it was shattered by an earthquake, with only the legs standing upright on the plinth. The huge head lay half buried in the earth, and the trunk was split open, revealing the webs of iron and the stuffing of stones. It was still lying there when Pliny came to Rhodes in the first century A.D. and examined the "dark caverns" of the fallen god. For some reason, when the Rhodians sent envoys to Delphi to ask whether the statue of Apollo should be raised, the oracle said it should be left untouched.

For nine hundred years the statue remained where it had fallen. Hellenism passed away, Byzantium rose, the Arabs emerged from the desert. In A.D. 677 a Jewish merchant from Emesa bought the statue from the local Arab commander. Apollo was cut into strips and three hundred tons of bronze were removed to the mainland. Then they were loaded on nine hundred camels and sent across the desert. No one knows what happened to them.

THE KNIGHTS OF ST. JOHN

As you enter the harbor at Rhodes in the blue morning air the battlemented walls shine like dusky gold, as pretty as toys. Windmills revolve along the mole, very white, their transparent sails catching the sun and throwing pale dappled shadows on the walls. There are only three or four windmills, but they have the effect of a forest of welcoming arms, and they turn very slowly, for only the faintest wind comes from Asia. The sea is a strange deep crystalline blue: the blue of ripening grapes held up to the sunlight. As far as the eye can see there are medieval castle walls, fortresses and battlements.

Entering the harbor of Rhodes on a clear summer morning is to know the wealth of the Middle Ages in a single glance. There are cities in Spain and France like Avila and Aigues-Mortes which are surrounded by medieval walls, but there is no other city which demonstrates so convincingly the power of the Knights who went out to defend the Holy Sepulcher and rejoiced in the opportunities of piracy they encountered on the way.

As the ship glides closer into the harbor, the walls are no longer toys. They have pride and beauty, and they have a human grandeur. Time has stood still. They do not melt like honeycombs in the sun, but they are the color of sun-warmed honey. They do not threaten. They have no purpose now except to keep out the wind and to provide a nesting place for birds. At sunrise and sunset and high noon they have the authority and dignity of ancient oaks. Their towering strength is allied with delicacy.

This honeycomb of walls is a thing to marvel at, for it is continually changing color: there is every kind of gold: gold fading to brown: gold shot through with black and green and purple in the evening fading light: and always this gold is patterned with the reflections of sea water, and therefore always in motion. Aigues-Mortes once stood by the sea, but its walls are coldly white. Only the façade of the Doge's palace at Venice can rival the walls of Rhodes; but there is a deliberate and patterned elegance which gives the Doge's palace the air of being contrived for the purpose of reflecting the sea to the best advantage. The walls of Rhodes are not contrived. They are the logical descendants of the walls which guarded ancient Mycenae. Remove the sea, set them on some deserted plain in Apulia, and they would look stern and beetle-browed. They smile because the sea smiles on them.

For close on four centuries Rhodes has suffered no alteration, and you can still walk through the streets which the Knights of St. John would recognize as their own. Those curtains, gates and towers, those innumerable turrets and mullions, gargoyles and emblazoned façades, belong to a world which has passed, but how effortlessly they weave their enchantment over us, how easily we find ourselves assuming the habits of composure and meditation which go with living in a walled city! The famous Street of the Knights is formed of two rows of stone palaces leading up to the palace of the Grand Master on the brow of the hill. The stone absorbs the sound of footfalls. It is very quiet, and the sound of someone playing a piano in one of the remote recesses of one of those palaces comes like an outrage.

For four centuries Rhodes has slept. Before that, it was one of the

places on the earth which proclaimed vigilance as its watchword. It
was a shield surrounded with eyes. It was armed to the teeth, and
from every lookout on every wall men searched the sea for the trace
of an enemy. It was the last bastion of the West against the threatening
East.

In 1306 the Genoese admiral of the Byzantine empire sold Rhodes,
Cos and Leros to the Order of St. John of Jerusalem, then established
on the island of Cyprus. Rhodes became the headquarters of the
Order, which consisted of Knights, Brothers and Clerks organized
into eight "tongues." These in order of precedence were the "tongues"
of Provence, Auvergne, France, Italy, Aragon, England, Germany
and Castille; nearly all the administration of the Order fell into the
hands of the French, who outnumbered the others. The Knights built
the great cincture of walls, and under the Grand Master Pier d'Au-
busson they successfully resisted the assaults of Sultan Mahomet II
in 1480. Forty-two years later Sultan Suleyman the Magnificent decided to put an end to the power of the Knights, who were openly
aiding the Christian corsairs raiding the coast of Asia Minor. He
brought up an army of 150,000 men in 300 ships. There were only
600 Knights and 4,500 mercenaries. The siege, which began in June,
1522, lasted for six months, and the defenders surrendered only when
they were so reduced by starvation and disease that they could fight
no longer.

The siege resembled the siege of Constantinople. There, too, a
handful of dedicated men had held up a vastly superior army of the
invaders.

It began with a concentrated broadside from more than a thousand
guns mounted on the ships in the harbor. Rhodes burned, but the fires
were put out. For three months the Knights succeeded in keeping
the Turks from penetrating the walls. Finally, on September 24, they
succeeded in breaching the walls of Aragon for exactly three hours,
when they were forced to retire. Suleyman, who was present on his
flagship, asked for the casualty lists, learned that 15,000 men had been
lost in order to make a temporary three-hour breach in the walls, and
spoke about lifting the siege. Later that day, according to the legend,
there was handed to him a message borne on an arrow from the Grand

Chancellor Andrea d'Amaral, the titular head of the "tongue" of Castille, who had hoped to become Grand Master and was therefore the inveterate enemy of Villiers de l'Isle-Adam. The message revealed the desperate straits of the besieged, with almost no food, and ammunition running out. Suleyman decided to prosecute the attack with even more vigor.

D'Amaral's valet and a Greek priest revealed the secret of the message sent to the Sultan. D'Amaral was arrested and given a drumhead court-martial. He was beheaded and quartered, and portions of his body were exposed on every bastion.

The siege continued. On October 10 the Turks seized the bastion of Aragon, but the defenders quickly threw up a new bastion in front of it. But they were at their last gasp. In November 29 the bells of St. John's Church pealed and the Greek Archbishop urged the people to the walls in a last superhuman effort to dislodge the Turks, but there was almost no strength left in them. For three more weeks the defenders held out, and then on December 22 the Grand Master surrendered to the Turkish Sultan, who rode into the city over the bodies of forty thousand Turks. Of the six hundred Knights who were alive at the beginning of the siege there were only some one hundred and eighty left alive.

The Sultan gave orders that the Knights should be treated with great courtesy; all honors were to be paid to them, and they were not to be ill-treated in any way. On January 1, 1523, Villiers de l'Isle-Adam, accompanied by the surviving Knights and five thousand Greeks who chose to go into exile with him, sailed for Malta. Rhodes became a Turkish city.

So it remained until the war between the Turks and the Italians in 1912; then for a short while the Italians took possession of the island. At the end of World War I they claimed the island as their own, and when Mussolini came to power, he set about restoring the palaces to their former grandeur. The Palace of the Grand Master especially pleased him. It was renovated from top to bottom, and every cranny of the palace was filled with paintings and Gobelin tapestries and gilded angels and overstuffed chairs and mosaics lifted from the neighboring island of Cos, until it became an example of how a palace should *not* be renovated. A special throne was imported from Italy for the use of the diminutive King Victor Emanuel III. In time the Italians under Mussolini conquered Albania and Ethiopia, and to celebrate the new imperial pretensions of Fascism, Mussolini ordered an inscription to be placed at the entrance of the palace. In large gold letters can be read the words:

REGNANDO SVA MAESTA
VITTORIO EMANVELE III
RE D'ITALIA E DI ALBANIA
IMPERATORE DI ETIOPIA
ESSENDO DVCE DEL FASCISMO
CAPO DEL GOVERNO
BENITO MVSSOLINI

The Greeks have not troubled to remove the inscription. It amuses them to observe that grandiloquence, which seems to belong to an age even more remote than Demetrius Poliorcetes, the Knights of St. John or the conquering Turks.

There are still Turks in Rhodes, and from the minarets of the mosques at sunset there comes the soft call of the muezzin over a Gothic city. In quiet gardens shaded by palm trees the mullahs walk, as they walked in the time of Suleyman the Magnificent; and the tombstones with stone turbans lie close to the tombs of the ancient knights. In every street there are Turkish fountains of blue tiles with Arabic inscriptions. Little has survived from ancient Greece—a few columns of a temple to Aphrodite, a ruined temple to Apollo, stone dolphins and lions and sepulchral monuments in the museum, in the hospital of the Knights of St. John.

Among these relics of Greece is a breathtaking Aphrodite dredged up from the sea. She stands there among the heaps of cannon balls and the geometric vases, carved from Naxian marble, very white, very pure. For countless centuries the sea has been busy softening the lines of her belly, smoothing her breasts, removing from her face all the features of youth and putting in their stead the anonymous features of an immense old age. There is a rust-red stain over her heart, where perhaps for ten centuries there lay the heavy ropes of an iron anchor chain; and a great wedge has been taken from her buttocks. Armless and faceless, with her curls in place, deflowered by all the creeping things of the sea, and virginal still, she rises in perfect grace and nakedness, the loveliest Aphrodite who ever rose from the waves.

THE TEMPLE ON THE CLIFFS

There are no roads in Greece so charming as the road which leads from Rhodes to Lindos, on the southeast coast of the island. It is one of those roads which seem to have been designed for the sole purpose of giving pleasure. You leave the gardens of Rhodes and enter a broad valley where the blue mountains glitter in the sun, and there is so much freshness and effervescence in the air, so much expression on the faces of the village children, so many flowers and so many green fields that you are in danger of resolving to stay on the island forever.

The road seems to have been artfully arranged to provide exactly the right approach to Lindos. It follows a wild coast, swings inland, climbs over the pass at Archangelos, where the women wear high leather boots, and suddenly, after wandering over low hills, it plunges down to the sea. There before you, rising abruptly between the shining waters of two bays, is a great headland crowned with the pillars of an ancient temple to Athene.

Nothing like this temple exists anywhere else in Greece. Imagine the Acropolis at Athens placed on the edge of a high cliff overlooking seas of the darkest, the richest, the most superb blue which has ever been painted. Imagine an atmosphere of exquisite luminosity, the air reflecting the depths upon depths of blue light flung upward from the sea. Imagine that all round this yellow headland there should be the visible signs of every period of Greek history. Imagine a quiet village paved with black and white pebbles at the foot of the cliff, shady courtyards, palm trees, cool churches in narrow lanes where the gold icons gleam, and pleasant eating places under the shade of trees. Only then will you have some idea of the extraordinary beauty of Lindos.

After journeying all over Greece and visiting all the islands, Lindos is the place to come to in the end. Here is refreshment enough for anyone weary of traveling, and more beauty in the space of an hour's wandering than one is ever likely to see.

Lindos has its place in history. At some remote period in the past, Danaüs and his fifty daughters fled to this promontory after escaping from Egypt, and built the sanctuary of Athene in honor of their safe landfall. On the walls of the temple of Athene, Pindar's hymn in honor of Diagoras was engraved in letters of gold. St. Paul entered the bay below the cliffs. The Knights of St. John built a fortress on the acropolis. The Turks built a mosque. It was Cleombulus, tyrant of Lindos, one of the Seven Sages of Greece, who first announced the words which pleased Apollo so much that they were engraved on his temple at Delphi: "Nothing in excess." On a bare rock below the cliffs lies the tomb of the forgotten sage, of whom we know only that he traveled in Egypt, wrote thousands of verses and was reputed to be very beautiful. It is a name to roll on the tongue. In those parts of Provence which were founded by Rhodes the name of Cléombule can still be heard.

At the foot of the cliff there is a relief of a ship with three banks of oars, which may have been carved by the ancient Phoenicians. On the way up to the acropolis we come upon a Byzantine fortress guarding the approaches to the temple, turrets and battlements still in place. Transformed into a castle of the Knights, it still wears their heraldic emblems; and on the cliff edge, clinging to the rock, stands the ruined Byzantine church reached by a narrow and treacherous stairway restored by the Turks. But it is the platform with its columned porticoes, archways, steps and pathetic remnants of the once-towering temple of Athene which holds the eye and demands the tribute which we pay to the supremely beautiful. Those golden columns are purely Dorian. They have power and elegance. Against the indigo sky they shimmer and tremble, and seem about to soar into space. They represent Athene winged, the ever victorious, inhabiting the mysterious region between sea and sky.

All is treacherous here. Step back a few paces, and you fall four hundred feet over the cliff edge, to be dashed to pieces on the fuming rocks below. A French archaeologist stepped back to admire the columns a month before I was there, and the villagers say his body was never found. A German photographer suffered the same fate recently. Athene demands her sacrifices still.

This temple on the high cliffs is a perilous and holy place. Once there were bronze and gilded statues surrounding it, glinting in the sun, but now there are only the stone pediments with the sockets and the stains of rust where the clamps held the statues down. An immense statue of Athene wearing a gold helmet and leaning on her golden spear once guarded the entrance to the temple. Now the platform is bare except for the columns and the seabirds and the bees who have their combs in the rocks. Even in its greatest days, when it was gilded and painted, the temple cannot have been as beautiful as it is now. We see it as it was in the beginning, stripped to the bone, before the decorators went to work.

There is only one stairway on the northern face; the other sides fall sheer; and there is about this massive promontory, like a great shoulder rising from the sea, the suggestion of inviolate power. An immaculate beauty rules here. There is power of a kind that does not appall; it speaks quietly and with absolute certainty from the high place. Wearing her blue robes, crowned with the sun, Athene rules here still, surveying the world from her throne in Lindos. She has reason to be pleased, for the most august of temples has been erected in her honor.

THE FACE OF HOLINESS

The *Queen Frederica* is a kindly ship, calling in at all the Mediterranean ports and taking her time before returning to New York. In her leisurely fashion she coasts along the shores of Sicily, putting in at Messina, which was founded by Greeks, and then at Naples, the "new city," which sometimes looks as though it were the oldest city on earth, and then at Nice, which is Greek for "Victory," though no one any longer remembers what victory was celebrated here. As Greece and the Greek names vanish into the distance, the light grows darker and thicker. By the time you are sailing through the Straits of Gibraltar you become aware that the strange translucent shimmering radiance which hovers over the Greek islands has completely vanished.

The light thickens, the air grows stale, and gradually the memory of Greece fades. Can it be possible, we ask ourselves, that we have walked in the divine light? Why are there only a few places on the earth where the sunlight trembles and quivers, and encloses thoughts as well as people in an intoxicating radiance? Was it the light streaming from the face of Apollo which threw the ancient Greeks into their turmoil and sent them questing through time and space for the answers to the questions they were the first to ask? Were they closer to the fountains of life than we are, and therefore more clear-sighted? The ancient gods still walk across the hills of Greece and Italy and southern France. Why did they die upon the coasts of Spain?

So one wonders, while the ship skirts the Azores, and the atmospheric pressure falls, and there comes the strange uneasiness which is known to all returning passengers from Europe. For a few hours or days everything becomes damp, sleep becomes nearly impossible, and the baffled mind is turned in upon itself. The sweating air is full of contagious violence. There is nothing to be done but pace the deck and dream morosely about the unattainable brightness, the white islands in the blue seas, the air washed clear every day by the kiss of Apollo.

Even without the sudden climatic disturbance near the Azores, there are causes enough for irritation. Greece tells us how much we have lost. We depend upon our heritage more heavily than we realize, and somewhere along the journey we lost our way. We can no longer build temples which speak with the authority of the Parthenon, or create sculptures which define the human majesty as superbly as the figures on the pediment of the Temple of Zeus at

Olympia. We have no modern mosaics as great as the mosaics at Daphni, nor does it seem that philosophy has progressed an inch since Socrates asked questions in the shadow of the Acropolis, insisting on answers. Look into the jewelers' shops on Fifth Avenue, and compare our modern jewelry with the blaze of earrings and necklaces found in Greek tombs, or the still more majestic earrings and necklaces found in the five-thousand-year-old graves of Ur of the Chaldees. Our silver money is pale and flat compared with the coins minted in Greece. Our clothes are no improvement on theirs, and our public buildings are stale copies of their temples. We have thrown a dart at the moon and can send missiles ten thousand miles with deadly accuracy, but we have not learned to live with ourselves abundantly and nobly.

The great philosopher Heraclitus was once interrupted by visitors who came to his hut. They found him warming himself over his stove. When they held back and hesitated, Heraclitus smiled and beckoned to them, saying: "Here too the gods are present."

For the Greeks the whole world was a divine field, and men were only a little less than gods. The Greeks knew that without the knowledge of the divine presence life loses its savor, falls into the artifices of corruption, and turns into nightmare. They remained faithful to their gods because to do otherwise was to lose faith with themselves. When St. Paul declared: "Where no law is, there is no transgression," he was proclaiming a universal truth well-known to the Greeks: unless we live under a divine law, then all crimes are permitted to us, and all art is meaningless, and all purposes are vain.

There came a time when the Greeks knew their gods were dying. Plutarch, who was a priest of Apollo in his temple at Delphi, tells the story of the sea captain Thamos who sailed from Greece to Italy in the days of the Emperor Tiberius and heard at midnight a cry upon the waters: "The great god Pan is dead!" Suddenly the whole of nature began to weep over the death of the god.

But the gods never die. In the long history of the Greek gods there is no record of a god completely dying, for some relic of him survives. His influence spreads out like the ripples of water when a stone is flung in a pool, and his energy is bequeathed to his successor.

The Greek gods left a deep impress on Christianity. We have seen
how the Zeus of Phidias at Olympia survived in the Pantocrator at
Daphni. In a hundred different ways the imagination of the Greeks
served to shape the purposes of Christianity. So we find in the cata-
combs the young Christ depicted as Apollo holding his lyre. Compare
the Baptism of Christ at Daphni with the solemn awakening from
the waters of the divine Aphrodite on the Ludovici Throne. Fifteen
hundred years separate them, but they share a similar beauty of form
and a similar exaltation; they breathe the same air, and the same
waters flow over them. A few yards away from the Ludovici Throne,
in a little alcove in the Museo delle Terme in Rome, there is another
Greek sculpture of tremendous power. For some reason it is usually
described as the head of a sleeping Maenad—*una testa di Furia ad-
dormentata*. She is not sleeping, but lies there in the perfect calm of
ecstasy. It is a head of the purest majesty, heavy with vision, very
composed, with one eyelid flickering as though she were about to
awake. Compare this head, which was sculptured by Scopas about
395 B.C., with the head of the Virgin Crowned by Botticelli, and you
will see how the Greek gesture continued across the centuries to
assume a Christian form. Greek art and thought so penetrated Christianity that they became inseparable.

One day at a banquet Socrates related the strange utterances which
he put into the mouth of a priestess from Mantinea, though the words
seem to have been his own. The priestess was speaking of the perfect
life, the only life fit for men on this earth.

"This, my dear Socrates, is the life above all others that men should
live, meditating on perfect beauty. Once you have beheld that beauty,
you will know that it cannot be measured against gold or costly
raiments or handsome boys or youths. What if men had eyes to see
this perfect beauty—I speak of the divinely beautiful, which is pure
and clear and undefiled, untouched by the corruptions of mortality
and the colors and vanities of human life—what if a man should hold
that purest beauty in his gaze?

"Therefore I say that when he beholds this beauty with the eyes
of his mind, he will be able to create the reality of perfect beauty,
not the mere image only, and having created it and nourished true

virtue, he becomes the friend of God and is as close to immortality as any man can be."

This vision of perfect beauty is the particular contribution of Greece to the Christian tradition. Without it we are nothing. The vision implies that men should live abundantly and nobly in cities that are worthy of them, and with a sense of awe before the ghostly beauty of the earth. In the *Iliad* the anger of Achilles is "terrible as the morning star"; that was how the Greek imagination worked. They saw in the morning star a terrible divinity, who was very beautiful. They saw holiness wherever they walked. They saw it in little things. It was in the girl singing in the cornfield and in the young woman going down to the well and in the child riding for the first time on his father's shoulders; and there was the same holiness in the shape of the Parthenon, for that too was beautiful.

Holiness must come again; it has been too long from the earth. That is why for many generations to come men will return to the springs—to the splendor of Greece and the shattering light rising over the snow-white island of Apollo.

INDEX